Surfing human creativity with AI
—A user's guide

Nao Tokui

Preface

This book is informed and inspired by my own observations, experiences, extrapolations and conjectures, gained from working as a musician, surfer, and AI researcher. I wrote it as a guide to productive coexistence with AI for the general reader, based on my journey, the examples of others in the field, and a history of "creative disruption" in art and music, and creative uses of technology. I am personally and professionally optimistic about the potential of AI to augment human creativity and productivity, and I want to share how I came to that enthusiasm.

I grew up with a gap between my profound love for music and my inability to play the piano. I took lessons. I practiced. But music didn't flow from me as I'd hoped. The will was there, but some element was missing. Later in life, I found other non-traditional musicians who had forged alternative strategies: people like Brian Eno, DJs, and media artists. In the end, the QWERTY keyboard, and Artificial Intelligence (AI), enabled me to explore my musical talent and to teach me about the nature of creativity more efficiently than the piano keyboard had.

I also grew up with a love of logic puzzles and computers. Computers can solve calculations far more quickly and accurately than any of us ever will, and in doing so they can help speed us to fresh new ideas and insights. We call computers thinking machines, but I would argue that they are better described as mind mirrors, good for providing fresh perspectives on thinking, and for accelerating problem-solving. Once I started making music with computers, new worlds were revealed to me. A computer can no more replace a human thinker than a drum machine can replace a human drummer. Yet a drum machine can open a portal to an entirely other set of possibilities, which can teach us new things, both about the distinctive value of human intelligence, the unique contributions of human drummers, and the production of computer rhythms.

As someone whose talent, and career, were empowered by AI, I feel a sense of crisis about how people are discussing it. Considering human creativity superior is ludicrous. Ours was never the only creativity on Earth. AI is science, technology, and engineering. We are incredible in that we can think, but thinking, as such, means little without being codified into action. The history of science is a history of inquiry. Faced with rapid technological change, the best thing we can do is think and be honest and adaptive about our strengths and weaknesses. Smart creators know how to ask good questions. Examined in the right way, one can see myriad forms of creativity, including human, and non-human, many of which AI is already well on the way to acquiring. Machines can, and increasingly will, exhibit some forms of known creativity, and should continue to become ever increasingly facile at modeling undreamt-of others. Whatever creativity AI does generate should be substantially different from human creativity, yet at the same time help us understand our own creative strengths and weaknesses. AI is helping us build a much greater creative toolbox. Exploring creativity using AI will therefore help us come to a richer understanding of AI's possibilities and limitations, as well as an understanding of our own. When birds see airplanes, should we imagine that they condescend among themselves that "those machines can't really fly, because they don't flap their wings," or should they rather be in awe at a power so similar, yet so different? We should similarly be studying this new form of intellectual flight, to gain insights into new physics understandings and the wonder of motion, and in the process expanding our knowledge and awareness gained from the amazing new places it might take us.

And yet, back here in the present day, the press is filled with hyperbole — "AI is infallible," "AI is useless," or "AI will steal our jobs" — any of these statements can, and have been, easily disproven multiple times, and yet these zombie fears return, time and again. Firstly, AI fails constantly. This doesn't mean it hasn't already proven itself invaluable. Yes, AI will impact society, for better and worse. Social and economic researchers have their work cut out for them, developing new ways to deal with Keynesian "technological unemployment," but AI itself has no opinions at all, much less the mens rea to steal anything. "Essential workers" in a pandemic were the inviolable infrastructure — energy, water, air, food, transport, communications, medical, maintenance and repair, religious and social services. The question we should be asking is "Who are the essential workers in an AI economy, and how do we become them?"

This book was written for a general audience. The reader will not need specialist AI knowledge to enjoy it, though certain technologies will reoccur within it. Minimal technological explanations will be provided, hopefully without burdening the narrative flow. Ideally, it will have a shelf-life of years, not weeks. Where long-standing principles still serve I will happily use them, I will also introduce the latest research, and definition-challenging artworks. As an artist myself, I am naturally drawn to examples of creation employing AI that I feel reveal completely new aspects of art, music, and design. I hope that, by seeing them through the lens of AI creativity, the reader will come to understand how statements like "AI will steal designers and artists' jobs" and "AI is a tool to increase efficiency and with no added creativity" both miss their marks.

As a communications professional, I want this book to offer perspectives that you can put to work. Many fields may imagine that AI, or creativity, have little to do with them. I would ask those readers to imagine traveling back in time to the late 20C when people were saying their work didn't have anything to do with the Internet. There are few businesses in the developed world today which are completely unrelated to the Internet. I'm convinced that AI will become the same kind of core technological environment: a given, something essential. This book attempts to reinterpret artistic and managerial thinking from a machinic perspective.

Last but not least, I want my fellow AI researchers and engineers to read this book. It is my great hope that you might be surprised by the gap between your presumptions about AI and what's written here. I hope I can spark new perspectives on how we all see AI technologies. In my opinion, a greater variety of perspectives will eventually contribute to better AI technology development for all.

What follows is the general outline:
Chapter 1 establishes a sense of shared situational awareness about "thinking machines," and how art can be used to prove our understanding of creativity and AI.
Chapter 2 defines creativity from AI's perspective, modeling searches, citing creative biotic development that proceed from simple to complex as a result of system formation and feedback.
Chapter 3 reviews the history of mimicry in the service of expanding human creativity.
Chapter 4 examines the influence of AI/automation on creative practices, rights regimes, and authorship.
Chapter 5 postulates how to creatively deal with AI, based on the author's experience.

About the author

I was born in 1976, in Ishikawa Prefecture, on the West coast of Japan. I received my Ph.D. from the University of Tokyo. My doctoral thesis was on Human-Computer Interaction using AI to enhance human creativity, researching music-generating algorithms (sets of rules defining how to perform a task or solve a problem) combining Artificial Neural Networks (ANN) and evolutionary computing. I wasn't originally musically "gifted." My attempts to learn piano in elementary school had come to naught. I could neither play nor write music. Encounters with inspiring artworks led me to imagine how to augment my creativity using AI. I learned to generate feedback by working as a DJ, AI musician, and media artist. AI helped me realize my dreams.

Table of Contents

Preface — 02

Chapter 1: AI cannot be an artist. — 07

1.1 To make is to understand — 08
1.2 Pictures drawn "by" AI — 15
1.3 AI Intention and execution — 22
1.4 AI is more than a tool — 25

Chapter 2: The Library of Babel
—— Thinking about the nature of creativity through AI — 31

2.1 Creation and the Library of Babel — 32
2.2 Creativity from a computer's perspective — 38
2.3 Text generation by AI — Burroughs, Bowie, and GPT — 43
2.4 Performance generation, sound generation, procedure generation — 50
2.5 "Machines Can Produce Nothing"? — 19C AI — 56
2.6 Evolution and creativity — A Genetic Library of Babel — 62
2.7 For AI to generate its own creativity — 70

Chapter 3: A history of AI, simulacra, and simulation — 81

3.1 Edison's Turing Test — 82
3.2 (AI Hibari Misora) Doppelgangers and Impersonators — 87
3.3 A failure to replicate changed global pop — 90
3.4 Photography and painting — Imitation ≥ flattery — 94
3.5 The painter whose art was a mirror he himself was inside — 101

Chapter 4: AI Aesthetics
——The impact of AI on expression — 109

4.1 The Peacock's Tail — Optimization pitfalls — 110
4.2 Sinatra doo be doo be no do no K-POP — 117
4.3 "Seeds" over "artifacts" — The dissolution of fixed "works" — 122

Chapter 5: Tips for working creatively with AI — 135

5.1 Connecting disparate phenomena — 136
5.2 Cultivating the uncanny — 143
5.3 Embracing heterogeneity — 151
5.4 Value misconversion — 156
5.5 Tips for creatively interacting with AI — 162

Afterword — 169

Chapter ——— 1

AI cannot be an artist

1.1
To make is to understand

"Thinking machines" and AI

What is AI? My first day at the University of Tokyo AI laboratory, a senior researcher joked that "The first thing to remember about AI research is the constant need to redefine what AI is." I'd personally phrase it as: "An attempt to imitate intelligence in living things, especially human beings, using computers."

The history of computing can be described as a parallel history of AI.

In 1936, at the tender age of 24, Alan Turing devised the first theoretical "stored program" computer model, the blueprint for every computer in existence today. His mathematical model of a "universal machine" could read and write symbols, on paper tape. Even today it remains the simplest invention capable of arriving at any computable sequence. All known laws of physics can be described in math, and therefore can be proven on a universal machine. A "Turing complete" system is a system of universal machine-compatible devices capable of communicating those results with one another; a means of connecting all computable sequences.

By 1943, Warren S. McCulloch and Walter Pitts wrote *A Logical Calculus of the Ideas Immanent in Nervous Activity*, the first paper describing simplified artificial "neurons" which "mimic the brain" — establishing the metaphor.

The computer architecture in most computers is called Von Neumann architecture, after its inventor, Hungarian Neumann János Lajos, anglicized John von Neumann. In his 1945 paper proposing it, he similarly anthropomorphized computer operations as "decisions," and "memory." People today don't think twice about using the word "memory" to describe recorded computer data, but there was a time when it must have been shocking to hear of a machine making "decisions" based on its own "memory."

In 1951, Professor Minsky and Dean Edmunds built SNARC (the Stochastic Neural Analog Reinforcement Calculator), the first artificial neural network, using 3000 vacuum tubes to simulate a network of 40 neurons. He also cautioned against what he called "suitcase phrases," using words like "memory" or "intelligence" as descriptors, because they first needed to be "unpacked" into component elements to be meaningful.

In 1949, Arthur Samuel, senior engineer in charge of developing the IBM 701, IBM's first mass-produced computer, wrote a checkers (draughts) playing program, which many consider an early form of AI. In 1953 Samuel wrote, in *Computing Bit by Bit or Digital Computers Made Easy*, "The digital computer can and does relieve man of much of the burdensome detail of numerical calculations and of related logical operations, but perhaps it is more a matter of definition than fact as to whether this constitutes thinking." The release of his AI checkers-playing program made headlines as a demonstration of advances in both hardware and programming, and caused IBM's stock to increase 15 points overnight. In 1959, Samuels coined the term "machine learning," which he defined as the "programming of a digital computer to behave in a way which, if done by human beings or animals, would be described as involving the process of learning." Whereas McCulloch, Pitts, Minsky and Edmunds had been working towards general-purpose learning "neural network" thinking machines, Samuel was interested in machines suited to very specific tasks. Samuel's program was meant to store, and then search, for examples of checkerboard positions which could be applicable to a given point in a game. "The computer plays by looking ahead a few moves and by evaluating the resulting board positions much as a human player might do," he wrote. This technique is still relevant today in the form of reinforcement learning.

But the term Artificial Intelligence was coined by Dartmouth mathematics professor John McCarthy in 1956 for the *Dartmouth Summer Research Project on Artificial Intelligence*, "to proceed on the basis of the conjecture that every aspect of learning or any other feature of intelligence can in principle be so precisely described that a machine can be made to simulate it."

In 1957, research psychologist Frank Rosenblatt at Cornell Aeronautical Laboratory in Buffalo, New York, conducted early work which culminated in the development and hardware construction of the Mark I Perceptron in 1960, the first computer that used a type of neural network simulating human thought processes to learn new skills by trial and error.

Early experiments with symbolic AI, or expert systems, were of humans creating precise rule-based procedures, algorithms, to model logic. They were working from describing logic, and how logic is derived, by modeling biological processes, in an attempt to understand "natural," presumably human, intelligence. As physicist Werner Heisenberg famously said, "What we observe is not nature in itself but nature exposed to our method of questioning."

The goal was Natural Intelligence, that which we perceive as intelligent in the natural world, evaluated in terms of how well and how efficiently something can adapt, improvise and learn new things – in a new and unfamiliar environments and against unfamiliar scenarios — and achieve specific goals. To explain, I have a potted plant on my desk and a dog sleeping by my window. The plant will, over multiple generations, present incredible expressions of resilience and adaptation, but in the time span of a given generation, it can only expect to respond to the light and nutrients provided by its context. The dog can reliably move to take as much or as little sun as it likes, as well as food and water from whatever available sources. The dog is dramatically more capable of communicating its will to other living beings. Both are living systems that use completely different forms of intelligence to draw increasing amounts of energy from their environments, and adapt and improve in new and unfamiliar environments. But on different time scales and levels of complexity.

The standard test for determining machine intelligence is the eponymous Turing Test. Originally created as the *Imitation Game*, it was a kind of double-blind party game, a test to see if someone could determine an "other" person's gender, based on their answers to questions. It is relevant that Turing was what today we might call gender non-binary. The *Imitation Game* was later re-purposed to see if someone could determine whether this "other" behind the double-blind was human or computer. In *Computing Machinery and Intelligence* (1950), Turing wrote "if a machine is capable of convincing a human that they are communicating with another human, then that should provide one proof that the machine was within the realm of what humans consider intelligence." You might say that the Turing Test was the original "in cyberspace, nobody knows you're a dog."

Intelligence and AI are constantly being remodeled and redefined. Logic can be proven, but intelligence is more difficult. And yet we seem to intuitively feel that we can discern the difference between the intelligent and the non-intelligent. Turing's repurposed *Imitation Game* has been so effective and so misleading because it challenges our intuitive sense of intelligence. Thus the joke in my colleague's recursive explanation: It is not that we are always redefining AI per se, but rather that the history of AI research is a history of attempts to distinguish between what we consider intelligent vs non-intelligent behavior.

Another blind which keeps us from being able to grasp these intelligent machines is the constantly shifting scale of their capacity. According to Arthur C. Clarke's *Third Law*: "Any sufficiently advanced technology is indistinguishable from magic." Gordon Moore's "law" (or observation) stated that the number of transistors in an integrated circuit should double about every two years. This indicates that the computational power of computers increases by an order of magnitude every five years. The computers we have today are, therefore, one trillion times more capable than those first computers on which computational brains and modeling "intelligence" were imagined, and will soon be one quadrillion times more capable. And as of 2018, (current president and CEO of Nvidia Corporation Jensen) Huang's Law suggests that new architectures and methods of designing and implementing those transistors will continue to accelerate the development of AI for the foreseeable future. As of 2018, Huang's Law has superseded Moore's Law, which noted that processing should now triple every two years. AI, and this sense that it resembles "magic," seems to be only speeding up.

As we approach computers which are one trillion times more capable, on our way to one quadrillion times more capable, the question is "when will AI evolve something equivalent to sentience, where it can learn any task that a human being can?" This state is called General Intelligence. It's when roles will switch. AI will be us, and we will be the dog. And that is predicted to be followed by Super Intelligence, when our relative intelligence should be more like the potted plant. The good news is that this is all speculative. At the time of this writing, according to Facebook's top researcher, Yann LeCun, our best AI systems are still somewhere between the potted plant and a house pet.

In May 1951, Turing appeared on a BBC radio discussion program and was asked his thoughts about the question *Can Digital Computers Think*? His response was "it seems that the wisest ground on which to criticize the description of digital computers as "mechanical brains" or "electronic brains" is that, although they might be programmed to behave like brains, we do not at present know how this should be done." "The whole thinking process is still rather mysterious to me, but I believe that the attempt to make a thinking machine will help us greatly in finding out how we think ourselves." And this, to me, is a central insight in information technology. The idea is that computers are like mirrors, tools for accelerating the models we're able to derive based on what we're looking at: What intelligence consists of, and how it functions.

AI models Alternative Intelligence(s)

One way to describe AI is as mathematical models arrived at through trials. Once trials have proven successful, we can say that another form of AI exists and another tool has entered the AI toolbox. I sometimes imagine that each new successful trial indicates another possible art form!

We speak of Weak AI and Strong AI. Weak AI has pre-determined limited functionality, such as image recognition and voice recognition. Strong AI, on the other hand, is more versatile and capable of behaving like a human being. Currently, the AI we encounter in our daily lives is Weak AI. Strong AI systems which would exhibit human-like behavior are hypothetical, and even experts are divided on whether such a thing is fundamentally achievable.

Regardless of the exact technology behind the AI system, once it successfully produces some repeatable kind of intelligence, we tend to no longer consider it "intelligent" or threatening. Take a thermostat, for example. "Intelligent" thermostats are sold as being AI-equipped and indeed do function on well-established algorithms. But nobody worries about "the rise of intelligent thermostats." Currently, huge public and private sector research investments are being made in autonomous driving technologies, reported as "AI" because it makes it easier to attract capital. Thirty years from now, in a world where autonomous vehicles have become commonplace, we may well think no more of them than we would "smart" thermostats. Still, some trials are perceived as threats when they succeed. Computer-aided Othello is already unbeatable. That "intelligence" already rose, conquered, and now we've simply dialed back so that we can keep up, and enjoy as entertainment. When IBM's Deep Blue defeated chess grandmaster Kasparov in 1997, and DeepMind's AlphaGo program defeated Lee Sedol in 2016, both entered the popular imagination as "AI" because of associations with electric brains, of consciousness. While AlphaGo excels at Go, it performs at a sub-toddler level at everything else. Yet it captured public imagination (and funding) because it seemed to demonstrate a competitive intelligence. This is the "AI dilemma" or "AI effect," that AI researchers play on a pitch where the goal moves with each goal scored, and the scorekeepers are often the public imagination. Our constant need to redefine is based on a varied set of factors.[5]

Strong AI is imagined as something like Stanley Kubrick's HAL 9000, from his film *2001: A Space Odyssey*, an autonomous thinking and behaving AI, capable of functioning among us, as our equal or better. True Strong AI (also called Artificial General Intelligence, AGI) will be that AI which appears to us as though it had consciousness. The path to Strong AI is imagined as starting from Machine Learning (ML), a subcategory of AI, based on the idea that machines should be able to learn and adapt through multiple iterations based on "training data," and then make predictions or decisions without being explicitly programmed to do so.[fig1-1] They should be able to step out from under our shadow. ML further breaks down into Supervised Learning and Unsupervised Learning. In Supervised Learning, data that corresponds to the "answer" is provided in advance. The AI model then trains to evolve its methods for arriving at these correct answers from the given inputs. In Unsupervised Learning, no correct answer data is provided. Useful rules are derived by the AI model directly from the input data. Clustering algorithms that group data according to characteristics discovered by the algorithms themselves is one of the most common examples of Unsupervised Learning. Deep Learning (DL) is an ML method based on the notion of Artificial Neural Networks (ANN). ANN feeds data back and forth in response to sample training data, generating algorithms in the process, in a rough analogy to memory creation in the brain's synapses. In ANN this takes the form of a system of weighting which increases or decreases the strength of each signal at connection as the system refines how to carry out a given task. The knowledge exposed to the deluge of information unleashed by the Internet and SMS-equipped smartphones

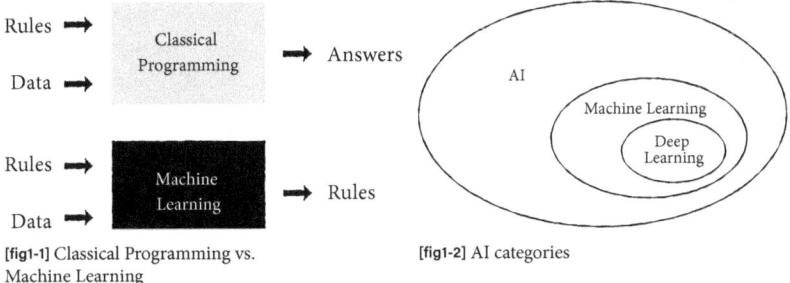

[fig1-1] Classical Programming vs. Machine Learning

[fig1-2] AI categories

from around 2010, and the development of GPU (specialized electronic circuits which rapidly batch-manipulate frame buffer memory, one key technology behind Huang's Law, above) architectures, have resulted in explosive innovation. ML and DL are our protagonists in this book.[fig1-2]

We have made a lot of fascinating tools to explore the nature of intelligence and to mirror the nature of intelligence. Our base assumptions and cultures are filled with various biases and flawed assumptions, including the belief that the world is primarily an anthropocentric domain. Science will develop according to sets of facts, which are abstracted to formulate hypotheses, so that experiments can be devised to test them, delivering a new updated set of facts. As Turing said at the beginning, regarding intelligence, "we do not at present know how this should be done."

I had the time to write this book because of a sabbatical created by a global pandemic in which AI played multiple critical roles in the discovery, development, and roll-out of vaccines. For at least the last 10,000 years, since the last major megafauna extinction, we have imagined ourselves essentially absent of significant predators. Our civilizations grew around the rules of our gods and our humans. And in recent years, not a few people have expressed concern about whatever potential threats AI might pose.

Is creativity what sets us apart?

According to a report by the Japanese Research Institute of Economy, Trade and Industry (RIETI), as of 2017, 30% of respondents in Japan indicated that they thought that their jobs were vulnerable to replacement by AI automation. The numbers were notably higher among the younger generation, with 42% of respondents in their 20s. A joint research project between the Nomura Research Institute and Oxford University in 2015 showed that 49% of the Japanese working population was vulnerable to replacement by AI and robotics, including logistics and factory workers, but also notably high-salary jobs requiring advanced degrees, socially respected white-collar jobs such as lawyers and surgeons. In Karel Čapek's *R.U.R.*, the robots were supposed to replace only the slaves.

So what sets us apart? One common answer to the question "what is essentially human?" is "creativity." Skills based on the ability to communicate with and inspire, namely artists, designers, and teachers are anticipated to be least vulnerable to AI and robotics, as we define each now, because AI is about detecting patterns, and creativity often implies novel ways of breaking patterns. And AI can help creatives keep up with the ever-increasing demand to produce more, faster. But is AI something that simply facilitates routine processes and not replacing us in creative positions? AI can mimic and replicate. But is it really incapable of proposing new creative options, alternative perspectives, that we wouldn't? I would argue that machines do have the potential for creativity, and it is important to understand what that creativity is and isn't. Moreover, AI creativity is substantially different from the creativity we humans are capable of.

Naturally, before speaking about AI and creativity, it's necessary to define what we mean by "creativity," not in terms of a deep dive into psychology or sociology, but rather as an attempt to provide a baseline for understanding AI in creative practice. Allow me to offer another Turing quote: "The whole thinking process is still rather mysterious to me, but I believe that the attempt to make a thinking machine will help us greatly in finding out how we think ourselves." This is the essence of my approach, paraphrased as "The whole creative process is still rather mysterious to me, but I believe that the attempt to make a creative machine will help us greatly in finding out how we ourselves create."

Attempts to model "creative machines" are attempts to deepen our own understandings of creativity per se, and to suggest a future in which creating machines go beyond being mere assistants, to contribute significantly to the expansion of human creativity, and beyond. If creativity is central to the essence of what it means to be human, then thinking about the future of human creativity and AI should lead us to consider the relationship between AI and ourselves. What relationship should we seek with AI? Let's start with some questions posed by artworks using AI.

[fig1-3] *AI: More than Human, Entangled Realities,* Barbican Centre

1.2
Pictures drawn "by" AI

The subjective in AI art

Accompanying the growing interest in AI technology is an interest in its cultural implications. In September 2017, the annual international media art festival Ars Electronica's theme was *Artificial Intelligence – the Other I* presenting over 600 different AI-themed events throughout Linz. From May to August 2019 the *AI: More than Human, Entangled Realities* exhibition held at the Barbican Center, London, featured many important artists from today's AI art world.[fig1-3] Also May to August 2019, the exhibition *Entangled Realities: Living with Artificial Intelligence* was held at HEK (Haus der Elektronischen Künste/House of Electronic Arts) in Basel. Following those, from October 2019 to February 2020, the Shanghai Ming Contemporary Art Museum (McaM) staged *Mind the Deep: Artificial Intelligence and Artistic Creation.*

Art exhibitions might strike some people as a narrow niche, but I would argue the contrary, that the freedom of artists and curators to work across disciplines and epistemologies give us an important cue about how we can approach this subject openly and historically, without getting bogged down in narrow debates about specific fields.

My experience of *AI: More than Human*, "an unprecedented survey of creative and scientific developments in Artificial Intelligence, exploring the evolution of the relationship between humans and technology" seemed the best representative of the problems of understanding AI and creativity.[6] Co-curated by British brand strategist and philosopher Suzanne Livingston and Japanese media art and design curator Maholo Uchida, the cultural differences between curators from island nations on opposite sides of the planet provided for a great breadth of perspectives. The show sought cultural context in history: Shinto Animist clay figures, Jewish Golem, and Frankenstein. The section on Mind Machines referenced the evolution of computing, from Charles Babbage's *Difference Engine* and *Analytical Engine*, through Turing's *Bombe* and *Enigma* code-breaking machines, and the relationship between calculation and thinking machines, to leading present-day creators. Perhaps due to the Barbican's role as one of Europe's leading culture centers, rather than a narrow inquiry into AI and creativity, it attempted to interrogate: "What it means to seek a non-natural intelligence?," "What is intelligence?," "What is consciousness?," "What is natural?," and "What is artificial?"

Let's classify this as existing on the continuum of "the constant need to redefine what AI is." Just as computers are machines created to mirror the workings of intelligence and therefore use anthropocentric words to describe them, the Barbican show continually returned to the idea that human achievement is a sum result of human will, an ancient search for intelligence culminating in this new artificial "intelligence" which effectively exists to replicate human intelligence. Of course, this is partially true, because that's what we have to start with. But rather than these replication steps being judged on their merits in the progress of providing AI tools for, and mirrors of, intelligence — whether that be plant intelligence or dog intelligence or simply rapid mathematical calculation — AI was here being examined in terms of "what it means to be human" or "will machines ever outsmart humans."

AI: More than Human saw over 90,000 visitors during its 3-month run. The opening event was so packed that I could hardly move. The majority of the *AI: More than Human* exhibition was used for exposition, for AI's technological background, the history of computing, from Babbage's Analytical Engine up to AlphaGo's beating Lee Sedol at Go. So although it was an art exhibition, there was also a strong pedagogic aspect to it. Jonathan Jones, a critic from the British daily newspaper The Guardian was scathing. His review *I've Seen More Self-Aware Ants!*[7] offered observations such as "*AI: More Than Human* does not actually prove that we're anywhere near the sci-fi future in which computers can think – or make art." "There's clearly no more "intelligence" behind them (Mario Klingemann's *Circuit Training* series exhibited at the show) than in a photocopier that accidentally produces "interesting" degradations." "Does the banality of the AI "art" here tell us anything about the state of AI itself? The question I'm left with is why so much is being invested in talking up the creativity of AI."

As a participant, I was first taken aback, but from Jones' critique I also sensed that the problem was partly that he entered having been sold an expectation that art could answer questions such as "What is Intelligence?" "What is consciousness?" "What it means to be human?" or "Will machines ever outsmart humans?" each of which would require artworks autonomously initiated by AI. In an interview, Klingemann clarified that in his AI work autonomy was never a consideration" …AI is just one tool in a long history of tools that was bound to be used for artistic purposes. But I would say I use AI as a tool and the works that I make with this tool are mine and not a collaboration, in the same way I would not call a hammer or a piano a 'collaborator.'"[8] It seemed like such a missed opportunity. Instead of serving to highlight where and how each AI artist was actually breaking new creative ground on a path to AI-assisted creativity, he was reviewing a battle between "thinking machines" and "creative" humans. This "creativity is what makes (us) human" trope, which I suspect informed his existential anxiety, places us in opposition to technological advances, and causes us to see them as threats.

In my field, music, the history of audio technology, whether struck or plucked or pneumatic tubed or electro-mechanical cylinder or wheeled, or even computer system generated, until quite recently instruments could still only play exactly as specified by a human. Or some subset of the same, like the "interesting degradations" Jones mentioned sometimes happen. In AI terms, music production had always been very Weak AI. Today's relatively Stronger AI, which has been trained on music data, can genuinely generate musical sounds which are unexpected without further human direction. When AI has been seamlessly integrated into our appliances, we may well call it automation. But increasingly, such automation will also be capable of autonomous contribution.

Paintings "by" AI

In October 2018, *Portrait of Edmond de Belamy*, [fig1-4] a picture submitted by IÉSEG School of Management business school students Hugo Caselles-Dupré, Pierre Fautrel, and Gauthier Vernier, going by the artist collective name Obvious promoted to this same ideal of an AI übermensch, "painted by AI," sold for $432,500 at Christie's, far above its predicted high-end estimate of $7,000-$10,000.[9]

GAN (Generative Adversarial Networks)[10] are a key AI algorithm right now, and will appear frequently in this book, so allow me to briefly explain. GAN is an example of unsupervised DL first proposed by Ian Goodfellow in 2014. It consists of two ANN, a Generator, and a Discriminator, which play an adversarial contest to identify patterns in training data without being given a clear correct answer, such as they would in supervised ML. [fig1-5] A set of data to be modeled, called training data, is provided. The Generator tries to fool the Discriminator by generating data similar to the data in the training set.[11] The Discriminator attempts to not be fooled, and accurately determine which incoming data are "true" original training data and which are the fake. Working together, they eventually become competent in reliably generating data identical to the training data.

The data set for *Portrait of Edmond de Belamy* was a set of 15,000 primarily public domain 14th-19th century European portraits, taken from WikiArt.[fig1-6] The GAN was trained on this data, the Generator learning to output patterns it had found in this dataset, and the Discriminator being fed both and learning to distinguish between images from the original data set, and those created by the Generator, like a duel between a forger (=Generator) and an appraiser (=Discriminator). Once the GAN was trained it could reliably generate 14C-19C portraiture-like images, theoretically endlessly. In fact, Obvious presented *Portrait of Edmond de Belamy* as one of a series of portraits of the fictional aristocratic Belamy family.[12] In the lower right corner, Goodfellow's mathematical formula for the GAN model was written by Obvious in place of the artist's signature.[fig1-7] It was clever marketing, as if to attest to the work's status as the first-ever original AI artwork. In interviews, Obvious furthermore stated, "The paintings were made by AI. We weren't involved in the production process." But is that true?

It is true to say that every single pixel in the image, every element of composition or coloring, was GAN model output as described in the bottom right corner "signature" formula. Every time Obvious pressed the enter button on their computer keyboard, the GAN model should have "automatically" generated a unique new "painting." And yet, without human agency to initiate the project, to organize the environment for learning, to set up the algorithm, and to curate the training data, the GAN algorithm or, therefore, AI alone, could never have generated any paintings. Obvious' evident obfuscation of the creation process, calculated misdirection designed to exploit common misconceptions about AI, and marketed to gullible collectors by Christie's, incited a storm of criticism from AI experts. *Portrait of Edmond de Belamy* was, if anything, specifically absent creativity, in AI terms, and furthermore, Obvious' contribution was very much less than presented in their auction dossier. Obvious were pretending to be pioneers, when this was not even the first example of an algorithmic artwork at auction. As it turns out, it's almost certain that Obvious didn't even curate their own original training data, but rather used source code already released on GitHub by then 19-year-old Robbie Barrat, including using his pre-trained modeling algorithms.[13] (Barrat has yet to receive any compensation from the sale.) The members of Obvious deny this, but it's easy enough to confirm by downloading Barrat's model and running it, generating paintings that are essentially the same "edition."[fig1-8] Obvious' primary contributions were in setting up their school computers and convincing Christie's. More central to our discussion, is the question of what is the appropriate

[fig1-4] *Portrait of Edmond de Belamy*

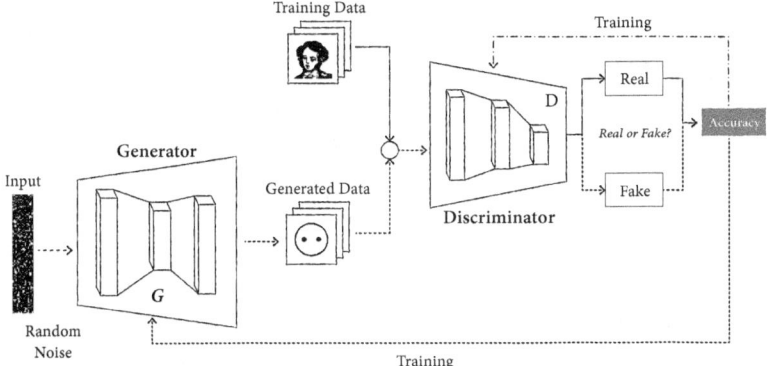

[fig1-5] GAN algorithm

[fig1-6] Portrait data opened for public by WikiArt.

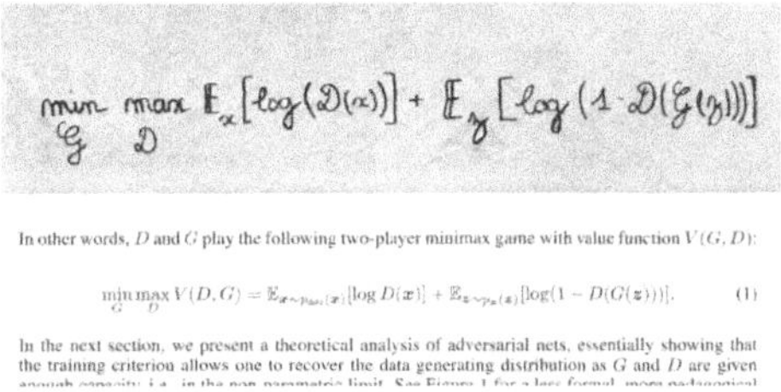

$$\min_G \max_D \mathbb{E}_x[\log(D(x))] + \mathbb{E}_z[\log(1 - D(G(z)))]$$

In other words, D and G play the following two-player minimax game with value function $V(G, D)$:

$$\min_G \max_D V(D,G) = \mathbb{E}_{x \sim p_{data}(x)}[\log D(x)] + \mathbb{E}_{z \sim p_z(z)}[\log(1 - D(G(z)))]. \quad (1)$$

In the next section, we present a theoretical analysis of adversarial nets, essentially showing that the training criterion allows one to recover the data generating distribution as G and D are given enough capacity, i.e., in the non-parametric limit. See Figure 1 for a less formal, more pedagogical

[fig1-7]
Above: Mathematical formula for GAN algorithm in place of the artist's signature.
Below: Mathematical formula on the original essay.

[fig1-8] An example produced by the author using Barrat's pre-trained model.

designation of authorship for *Portrait of Edmond de Belamy*? Is it the bourgeoise portraiture painter community from 14C-19C Europe? Or the curator who assembled those portraits and opened their license? Is it Goodfellow, through his GAN algorithm's invention? Is it Barrat, who trained Goodfellow's GAN architecture on those portraits, and released that source-code, with the pre-trained model on GitHub? Or is the trained GAN Generator that outputted the paintings? Or Obvious, who devised a way to make money from it all? To whom, or what, should the "creativity" be credited?

To me, the generous reading would be that Obvious' "creativity" is a misreading of conceptual art, or rather a prank on the art world, knowing how to prey on art world expectations and pretensions, and getting Christie's to present a work at auction without first determining provenance. Art, like AI, is a field of perpetually shifting self-referential definitions. AI cannot autonomously generate art without human agency now, nor will it be able to do so in the foreseeable future. Today's AI systems are all specific-purpose AI, highly targeted technologies that are useless for anything except precisely what they were created for. They don't have will, sensibility, or a sense of purpose like humans do. I don't know if ants are self-aware (and this is a topic we will turn to later), but I can say that they have more autonomy than any AI available today. What I want to propose is that dispelling that misconception is important, and does not mean that creating with AI is meaningless. Quite the opposite. Just as Art and AI are both fields with perpetually shifting self-referential definitions, and both are engaged in attempting to clarify how creativity and intelligence function. Hits and misses both will help us foster understandings. What is Art? What is creativity? What is AI? Can AI become creative? Where is the value of an artwork, when essentially similar "artworks" can be easily generated in limitless quantities using pre-trained AI models? What is our role in that circumstance? Obvious perhaps can claim to have been useful in, at least, providing us with material for these discussions.

1.3
AI Intention and execution

To make is to understand

In the one-in-a-million chance that Strong AI could ever achieve some form of consciousness recognizable to humans (something which we presently don't even have a way of understanding yet), then part of that should include will and a point of view which can be expressed. In such a scenario, Strong AI could become an artist. The art produced would logically be beyond human comprehension, like the art of an alien on a distant planet, unrelated to human universal grammar. Of course, theorizing about such Strong AI is only a thought experiment. But, the evidence, and common sense, suggests that should Strong AI emerge, it wouldn't turn on the computer one day and imagine "Fine day to draw a portrait series based on 14C-19C portrait training data," or "Once the AI has finished learning the 14C-19C portrait data set, then I can make an endless series of portraits of a fictional aristocratic family," or, by the way, consider "I wonder how much money and publicity I can generate if I can convince Christie's to put up this series for auction?"

As with early computer development, we needed to unpack "suitcase phrases" like "memory" and "intelligence," so with computer-generated creation, we must learn to unpack works like art and creativity. Both are difficult to define and likely change their definitions from person to person. If one thinks about the commonalities of paintings, sculptures, music, dance, and literature, of aesthetic sense perception, one will find the nature and appreciation of "beauty" and therein "truth," somewhere at the bottom of the "art" word suitcase.

According to art critic and philosopher Arthur Danto, 20C art, contemporary art was a transition away from "beauty" into a post-historiographic philosophical practice engaging signifiers of embodied meanings calling for interpretation, and that is what distinguishes art objects from other things in the world. Intent and execution are key.[14] Marcel Duchamp's *Fountain* (1917), presents an almost violent new conception of art, wherein the artist's intention and execution are prioritized over the entire craft tradition of "masterpiece" creation, dismiss-

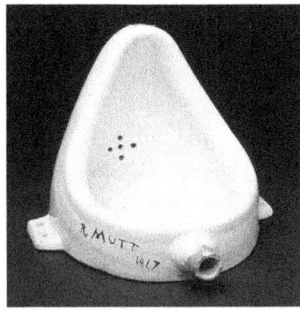

[fig1-9] Marcel Duchamp, *Fountain*.   [fig1-10] Google Clips.

ing the former as "retinal."[fig1-9] Yoko Ono's participatory practice, in masterworks like *Hide and Seek Piece: Hide until everybody goes home. Hide until everybody forgets about you. Hide until everybody dies*, in which the art making exists solely through the mutual conception of the artist and whoever feels motivated to complete the piece. Art is intent and execution, not form. And that is why the Ramones were never to be judged against Wolfgang Amadeus Mozart, and Duchamp and Ono only bring new depths to our appreciation of Da Vinci and Rembrandt.

What then is a useful critique for how human intelligence should apply these Alternative Intelligence(s) being generated in AI?

Pre-modern Fine Arts were traditionally examined in terms of elevated artisanal craft, whereas AI, etc., is quite the opposite — associated with automation. One way to bridge this gap would be to look at the role of automation in the fine arts, for which the rise of photography is perhaps the best example. The shutter mechanism, the exposure to film, and the developing process are the execution, automatically fixing an image on paper. Intention sets the subject, chooses the film, and exposure settings, and develops the resulting film. Nobody confuses the camera with the photographer, the tool with the artist. But as cameras, equipped with AI, begin to automate the shooting process: choosing the subject, and shutter timing, and producing successful results? At what point should we consider that the camera was expressing intent, and becoming the photographer?

Google Clips was "A hands-free (miniature clip-on) camera… that lets you effortlessly capture and view more of the spontaneous moments" according to the 2017 press blurb.[fig1-10] The presumed added value was that its ML AI would learn to determine "interesting" or "relevant" subjects. The promotional materials were filled with owners bursting into smiles, Google Clips having captured their pet's newest trick or their child's first steps, for example. The product didn't deliver and disappeared from the market within 18 months, after having sold only an estimated 15,000 units. But if Google Clips had succeeded and thrived, it's worth asking how its output would have differed from human photography?

One thing which would have been different from human photographers would be that the ML models and curated training data would essentially be co-authors of each photograph. Google Clips would have reduced human participation at the point of the shutter, but it wouldn't have erased human intention from the process. Photos taken by Google Clips might have been able to surprise their users, but it seems a stretch to call that "autonomy."

This question of autonomy seems key to this level of AI participation; whether in discussing Google Clips photography, AI word processing prompts, or Adobe Photoshop using a GAN model, none possess independent creative intent, and yet I think it's not wrong to credit them with some level of autonomy. Depending on how I engage my plant, depending on how I engage my dog, there might well be creative collaboration possible. And because AI models offer a marginally informed, directed unpredictability, elements of execution occur outside of users' original intent. AI offers a spectrum between simple tools and creative action. And this, I would argue, is where we might gain insights into extending human creativity: by granting AI a certain qualified sense of autonomy, even initiative. When we consider AI just a tool, we risk a mistake equal to or greater than imagining AI capable of autonomously producing art. AI will absolutely be able to solve whole classes of problems and provide different starting points for our intention and execution.

1.4
AI is more than a tool

Deviation tool

The statement "AI models are autonomous" is false. The statement "AI models are just tools" (so we're safe, because we're creative) is also false.

In 2019, the Japanese Society for Artificial Intelligence Ethics Committee, the Japan Society of Software Science Technology Special Interest Group of ML Systems Engineering, and other ML-related Japanese organizations released the joint statement "Machine Learning is nothing but a tool" as an attempt to assuage fears of an omnipotent AI and legitimize the primacy of humanity by fiat.[15]

A "tool" is an instrument or apparatus used according to human intent to amplify human ability. A hammer is a tool to use with nails and wood to make a house or a chair with more precision and complexity than we could otherwise. A piano is also a tool to use to convert tuned sounds into music with more precision and complexity than we could otherwise. Pianos didn't invent counterpoint, but the beautiful black-and-white symmetry in their interface certainly made picturing it easier. Paintbrushes are at the end of a long history of people wanting to fix their imaginations on surfaces, and paintbrush makers sit at the end of a long history of heuristic development, providing durability and a range of expression for whichever way the artist chooses to use them. But tools used in unconventional ways become something new. A hammer becomes a doorstop. A piano becomes a dais for family photos. Or a piano and nails can become elements of a "prepared piano" in the hands of John Cage.

AI for autonomous driving, facial recognition, and sound recognition processes are very particular and complex pre-determined tasks and must function as designed. Any variations from their designers' intentions are malfunctions. It's fine that they function as "tools," because there isn't any substantial disagreement between car manufacturers and driver safety objectives. Facial and audio recognition is pointless if they don't perform to standard.

But imagine a Strong AI creative suite of software far more advanced than today's. Maybe with a BCI (Brain Computer Interface) which allows the user to provide starting points, but then the AI might perform a series of complicated tasks, including generating visual and audio elements, output, and sharing them directly from the user's imagination. In that scenario, the user might have "created" the visuals and music, but their creation would have taken place entirely within the envelope of expressions — the definitions of sound and vision — defined by the affordance provided by the software company and AI engineers who developed it. The more advanced the tool is, the more difficult it would be to break free from the constraints of its design.[16]

With AI there will be superuser artist engineers like Mario Klingemann who can build their own systems, but absent such genius, most of us need to rely on strategies such as developing potential for creative misuse. AI is rejected in creative practice not only because it might replace workers, but also because AI might limit their affordance, effectively facilitating less creativity, and making them more subservient to clients, and software designers. Imagine the above scenario with the previous month's hit chart data plugged in, meaning that the "artist" can only produce "proven hit" melodies. How might we break free of these constraints?

Unique human creativity is often unleashed by first contact with new tools, and with aberrant and unintended uses. Glitches "in the matrix" can lead to exciting new places.

Hip-hop, a music genre with global appeal, was the product of misusing tools. The playing surfaces of vinyl records were not originally meant to be touched by human hands, because surface oil and dust are reproduced as noise.[fig1-11] And yet DJs pushing down on a vinyl record while moving it back and forth on a turntable to produce percussive or rhythmic sounds, "scratching" or "scrubbing" to a beat, initiated an explosion of new art forms. It might be described as an industrial accident, or sabotage. Originally, radio DJs would run records gently backwards to cue-up before a switch-over. After the Technics SL-1200 direct-drive turntable was released by Matsushita in 1972, DJs discovered that the motor would continue to spin at the correct RPM even if the DJ wiggled the record back and forth on the platter. The record player's "pitch adjust" function, originally designed to fine-tune the delay of rotation speed, came to be used to actively control the playing speeds and connect pieces of music with differing tempos.[17] Using two turntables, with a crossfader switching device between, a DJ could furthermore utilize the switch-over to apply interludes and rhythm breaks. Then rapping on top of that created the art forms of MCing, rap, and hip-hop. These innovations revolutionized music, dance culture, and club culture worldwide.

Most DJs these days have abandoned turntables and work off of laptops. But imagine if computers had gotten there first? Without turntablism, the bulk of club culture, and dance music in the world today

[fig1-11] Grand Wizzard Theodore invented scratch.

would not have come into existence. DJ Krush, godfather of atmospheric hip-hop, speaks hilariously of his early days DJ-ing on the streets of Harajuku, constantly being instructed by well-meaning passers-by, young and old, to please stop touching his vinyl or scratching it.[18] One can easily imagine DJ software developers proudly promoting "AI anti-scratch noise elimination functions!" to inhibit the "noise" produced when cue-ing up for a switch-over. Software can emulate scratch, but it would never have aimed for the same expressions. And it's not just for DJ culture. Neither Jimi Hendrix's "rockets red glare" amplifier feedback, nor Jackson Pollock's action paintings would have become our cultural inheritance if the expressive affordance of guitar or painting "tools" had been predetermined by software.

If, as Joyce's Stephen Dedalus says "History is a nightmare from which I am trying to awake," then the history of computers is a history of mind mirrors, explorations in modeling intelligence, to objectify thinking, and the data we base our culture on: a chance at examining thinking, and creativity rationality. Each new successful AI "trial" indicates another possible art form. Natural intelligence exists in a spectrum, from the plant on my desk, to the dog resting in the yard, to me at my desk, to other things still undiscovered. But if the natural intelligence of my plant, or dog, were to achieve an equivalent of Strong AI intelligence, there is no reason to believe that they would exist in a hierarchy beneath human intelligence. Strong plant intelligence might invent myriad art forms of forest canopy leaf patterns or flowers we can scarcely imagine. Strong dog intelligence might choose arts of smell and sound completely outside of our perceptual realm, and re-inform our musical culture. Similarly, post-singularity AI might choose art in forms of number sequences none of us will be able to grasp, etc. AI is the original multiverse of intelligences.

AI is just a tool, but it is also not just a tool. AI is a tool to the extent that everything meaningful will come out of our intent and execution in using it, and it is not just a tool because it will continue to articulate and offer more expressive possibilities. AI will not remain forever subservient to the artist simply because we wish it would, and minimizing discussions of this kind are both easy to legitimize and irresponsible. We need to quit mis-imagining AI and work on having a clear-eyed view of what AI can do for us, and with us. But I rarely hear that opinion. AI, as a tool in creative practices, has to be something that works with users' intent and not just the AI system designers' intent. A margin for "misuse" needs to be built-in. (Obviously, I'm speaking of "misuse" in terms of creative expressions, not for invasions of privacy or any other form of weaponization.) AI is not just a tool, because it has a certain sense of autonomy.[19] This is not to say that AI already has intent, but rather to assert that what I find interesting about AI is that it combines a certain "intelligent" unpredictability, which pushes me as a creator to think further or beyond its designers, engineers, and users' original intent. The idea that the computer, or AI, cannot "originate anything" but only "can do whatever we know how to order it to perform" (Lovelace, 1842[20]) is an opinion as old as the invention of computers, and arguably rooted in a concern about human primacy. Can computers produce that which is new, unexpected, and valuable? A word processor should produce exactly what you've typed in. Klingemann and Obvious were no doubt counting on the unpredictability of what AI would propose to them. AI does generate possibilities, loosely based on outlines set out by the intent of its users, and therein unpredictable results. AI can be something to reclaim certain uncertainties, reassert unpredictability into software. Creative use of AI needs to function in the uncertain territory, between an object's resemblance to recognizably human elements and the emotional responses to it, somewhere between serving as a tool and as a mirror, to help us reflect on how rich intelligence can be. To the extent that AI does these things, AI is meaningful. We are the children of Homo Habilis, the tool-making ape. To borrow from Marshall McLuhan, "We shape our tools, and our tools shape us."[21] We will shape AI, and AI will shape us. AI will be developed to mirror us, and we will, in turn, mirror it. Our task is to approach AI in a way that leads to a richer, more creative individual, social, and cultural existence.

Endnotes

1. John von Neumann, *First Draft of a Report on the EDVAC* (1945)
2. Rodney Brooks, *The Seven Deadly Sins of AI Predictions*, MIT Technology Review (10.2017)
https://www.technologyreview.com/2017/10/06/241837/the- sevendeadly-sins-of-ai-predictions/
3. A.M. Turing, *Computing Machinery and Intelligence* (Mind, Vol.59 1950)
4. Huang's law is an observation in computer science and engineering that advancements in graphics processing units (GPU) are growing at a rate much faster than with traditional central processing units (CPU). The observation was made by Jensen Huang, co-founder, president and CEO of Nvidia.
5. Douglas Hofstadter once famously said "AI is whatever hasn't been done yet."
6. At the exhibition, I exhibited an interactive music piece called *Neural Beatbox* that my team at Qosmo and I worked on.
https://www.neuralbeatbox.net/
7. Jonathan Jones, *'I've Seen More Self-Aware Ants!' AI: More Than Human – review* (The Guardian 5.2019)
https://www.theguardian.com/artanddesign/2019/may/15/ai-more-than-human-review-barbican-artificial-intelligence
8. Martin Dean, *Artist Mario Klingemann on Artificial Intelligence, Technology and Our Future*, Sotheby's (2.2019)
https://www.sothebys.com/en/articles/artist-mario-klingemann-on- artificial-intelligence-art-tech-and-our-future
https://www.youtube.com/watch?v=Jjv3m5oWICA
Katharine Schwab, *The Future of AI Art goes up for auction at Sotheby's for $50,000*, Fast Company (2.2019)
https://www.fastcompany.com/90305344/the-future-of-ai-art-goes-up-for-auction-at-sothebys-for-50000
9. *Is Artificial Intelligence Set to Become Art's next Medium?*, Christie's.
https://www.christies.com/en/stories/a-collaboration-between-two-artists-one-human-one-a-machine-0cd01f4e232f4279a525a446d60d4cd1
10. Goodfellow, Ian, et al. *Generative adversarial nets.* Advances in neural information processing systems 27 (2014)
11. This sentence is a good example of our tendency to anthropomorphize AI.
12. The name Belamy was an homage to the GAN inventor: Goodfellow translated as "belle," and "'ami."
13. James Vincent, *How Three French Students Used Borrowed Code to Put the First AI Portrait in Christie's*, The Verge (10.2018)
https://www.theverge.com/2018/10/23/18013190/ai-art-portraitauction-christies-belamy-obvious-robbiebarrat-gans
14. Arthur C. Danto, *Remarks on Art and Philosophy* (2014, Marion Boulton Stroud), and 1984's essay *The End of Art*.
15. *Statement for Machine Learning and equitability* (12.2019)
http://ai-elsi.org/archives/888
16. François Osiurak, Jordan Navarro, Emanuelle Reynaud, *How Our Cognition Shapes and Is Shaped by Technology: A Common Framework for Understanding Human Tool-Use Interactions in the Past, Present, and Future*, Frontiers in Psychology (3.2018)
17. Originally called pitch adjust on early version of the Technics SL-1200, it came to be known as pitch control on models after the SL-1200MK2 released in 1979.
18. Katsuaki Hosokawa, *A portrait of the Technics SL-1200 — The turntable that started a revolution* (Rittor Music, 2019)
19. I use the word "autonomy" in a marginal sense, in that it simply operates automatically and contains certain unpredictability.
20. Mentioned in the second chapter.
21. This quote was actually written by MucLuhan's friend and colleague John M. Culkin, in a text introducing McLuhan's philosophy.
John M. Culkin, *A Schoolman' s Guide to Marshall McLuhan*, The Saturday Review (3.1967)

Chapter 2
The *Library of Babel* — Thinking about the nature of creativity through AI

2.1 Creation and the *Library of Babel*

Once upon a time, there was a library that contained every book ever written, as well as every possible permutation of every possible book which might ever be written. It was a galaxy of all possible books, encompassing all possible combinations of the 30 letters of the Roman alphabet, starting from abc, including the space, the question mark, etc. No two books were the same. One day I found myself lost in this library. I picked up a book at random from the shelves. It began "aatlewpukwhze p,uvtpqstymfhmpfb rteleaiswxu xxkouufdcg.opi djwn,prgjigdo,yldyhptnmrvvcejsa. xxchmx oihesl xsdckue bqsrbe," so I put it back. The next book began "nidfug joukdfa hguwa fkjda outrqd kjfafdas gldaop gj qdfa buiokdsjaf faqeq." I couldn't detect any rhyme or reason for the book order. Most of them were gibberish. With every possible permutation included, somewhere there had to be a book that started and ended with only "a," and another one identical except it ended with "b." Somewhere in the library, there should also be *Harry Potter and the Philosopher's Stone*, and *The Tragedy of Hamlet, Prince of Denmark*. And tomorrow's New York Times. And the day after's. I wandered the library, searching for esoteric titles, maybe *Harry Potter and the AI Necromancer*, or alternative English language translations of famous Japanese authors such as Soseki Natsume or Osamu Dazai. (As a library of books all written in the English alphabet, even though some might resemble the stylistic and symbolic "fingerprints" of various authors since they would have never originally existed in Japanese, should we even call them "translations?")

After searching for decades, one day I opened a book that began "This book is informed and inspired by my own observations, experiences, extrapolations and conjectures, gained from working as a musician, surfer, and AI researcher." The book that you now hold in your hands. I looked for the author's name — while wondering how could an author matter, whose concern could it be, who wrote which book, if every possible permutation of all books was already here? If we know that there is a finite set of all possible books, then anything is either a book already discovered or one that has yet to be discovered. Being who I am, I did take this book, leave the library, and claim it as my own. I presented it to a publisher who told me, "I've never seen a book like this.

[fig2-1] Left: *The Library of Babel*
Right: Drawing by Erik Desmazières

The topics tend to leap all over the place, but it fits the demands of the day. Let's publish it." And thus it came to be published.

But the question remained with me: What was "my" creative act? Was I the sole author of this book?

Of course, many readers will have noted that I am referencing *La biblioteca de Babel, The Library of Babel*,[1] first published in 1941 by Argentinian author and librarian Jorge Luis Borges.[fig2-1] Borges was born into a family who lived in a large house with a library, whose English volumes alone numbered over one thousand. Throughout his career, he worked in libraries; in 1955, becoming director of the National Library of the Argentine Republic, though ironically, by 1957, he had gone completely blind. The protagonist of this story is a librarian, born in a library that covers all combinations of letters, and within a society of fellow librarians, all of whom spend their lives searching the library looking for books that are more than assemblies of letters, rather books with actual meaning.[2]

As a practical matter, if you were one of these librarians, how would you go about searching for books with meaning? What are the odds that any random adventure into this library would produce one? Let's calculate the odds via the total possible number of volumes such a library would hold. If we assume a set of books the size of this one, all of the books are 400 pages, formatted at 80 lines per page, an average of 40 letters per line, each line. The total number of possible patterns in each line (repeated permutation) would equal 30 letters to the 40th power. This in itself would generate 121,576,654,590,569,288,010,000,000,000,000,000,000,000,000,000,000 patterns. This number to the 80th power will generate a page, and that number to the 40th power will generate one book. By these calculations, there should be 1.60×10 to the 1,890,715th power of different books. For comparison that number is, surprisingly, greater than the Eddington number, which is the number of protons in the observable universe, or 1.574×10

to the 79th power. Of course, most of the books would be gibberish. The set of books that exhibit any characteristics of grammar should be quite limited. As a set of the total number of already "discovered" books, Google researchers estimate there are about 1.3 x 10 to the 8th power, or 129,864,880 published books currently on Earth.[3] Therefore, against such astronomical odds, we must assume that when one of these librarians discovers a complete *Hamlet* or *Harry Potter*, or even one or more meaningful books in their lifetime, there must be a genius or a technique. Obviously, there is no library with more books than the total number of all protons in the observable universe. To the extent that each book consists of particular letter combinations, the total number of possible combinations is enormous, but finite. In this metaphor, my job as author-as-searcher was to discover the book which corresponds to the arrangement of letters that spoke a truth I knew, and shed light on that, from among the myriad of other less true possibilities.

The *Library of Babel* thought experiment provides fertile metaphors for three importance aspects of creativity in AI:
1) A well-scaled task.
2) The search algorithm.
3) The evaluation function.

Let's look at each in turn. First off, I think it's fair to say that most people have an intuitive resistance to equating discoveringwith creating. Our image of creation has to do with grace, with imagination, with something emerging from nothing. We have questions, and criteria, which seek specific answers. But the *Library of Babel* provides an easy metaphor for imagining search,a well-scaled macrocosm of possible expressions can make discoverya form of creation.The first lesson would be to define an appropriately creative and large search spacebecause the ways in which the librarians' search space is defined will in turn help define their affordance of discovery. Starting with a book this size means a literally super-astronomical set of possibilities. Yes, if our *Library of Babel* were filled with only single paged books, it would be only of too-simple ideas. You need sufficient expressive potential within a manageable search space. It's important to set limits cleverly.

The *TR-808 of Babel*

To me, as a musician, the TR-808 Rhythm Composer can be described as just such a library. Manufactured by the Roland Corporation between 1980 and 1983, it was one of the first programmable drum machines, capable of producing 11 maximum simultaneous sounds including kick, snare, and hi-hat.[fig2-2] One musical bar can be set per sixteenth note, or 2 to the 16th power = 65,536 patterns. If you add all 11 tracks, there are 9.5 x 10 to the 52nd power of patterns. Originally criticized for its "unrealistic" drum sounds, it was discontinued after only 12,000 units had been sold. And yet, the TR-808 has been used on

[fig2-2] Roland TR-808

Pattern 1	1	2	3	4	5	6	7	8	9	10	11	12	13	14	15	16
Bass Drum	■				■				■				■			
Snare Drum					■								■			
Closed Hi-hat	■		■		■		■		■		■		■		■	
Open Hi-hat																
Cymbal																
Clap																

Pattern 2	1	2	3	4	5	6	7	8	9	10	11	12	13	14	15	16
Bass Drum	■			■							■					
Snare Drum					■								■			
Closed Hi-hat	■		■		■		■				■		■		■	
Open Hi-hat							■									
Cymbal									■							
Clap									■							

Pattern 3	1	2	3	4	5	6	7	8	9	10	11	12	13	14	15	16
Bass Drum	■								■							
Snare Drum								■								
Closed Hi-hat	■		■		■		■		■		■		■		■	
Open Hi-hat																
Cymbal															■	
Clap								■								

[fig2-3] Examples of TR-808 rhythm patterns.

---

more hit records than any other drum machine. Artists from Marvin Gaye, to Afrika Bambaata, Pharrell, and Diplo. Musicians have been "creating" from the TR-808's "library," "discovering" great rhythm patterns in this *Beatbox of Babel* for decades.[fig2-3]

The 2nd lesson we can learn from the *Library of Babel* is the importance of a search method, or algorithm. Even with a well-defined set of limitations, absent a method, the librarian still won't be able to discover any meaningful books. Therefore the existence of a wise search method, an algorithm, determines the librarian's productive capacity. If books are lined up in alphabetical order, for example, and the librarian starts from the beginning, repeatedly assessing "is the desired book before or after the randomly selected book in front of you?"[4] they should be able to discover something useful much faster than simply by checking each, at random.

Similarly, the music genres generated by the TR-808 might be described as products of distinct search algorithms. The librarian can always make rhythms from random combinations, like picking up a random book in the *Library of Babel*. But if you already have a cool rhythm (=algorithm) in mind, then you can start with that, and start creating deviations from it. For House music, the librarian only needs to start with kick drums on the quarter notes, and open hi-hats on the backbeat[5] to make a typical four-to-the-floor rhythm, and then explore from there. Dial into good rhythms, modify them slightly, or dial out. Assessing whether or not before the modification was better, and if so, then undoing the change, or maybe adding it to another place: This is a legit random search algorithm.

Another useful tactic might be to combine what you're doing with existing cool rhythms. Either way, you'll have better luck than by just programming at random.

But how do you judge if something is "good?" In order to search you need qualitative criteria in order to assess whether or not a given rhythm pattern is "cool" or "beautiful" or "interesting." This brings us to the 3rd lesson we can learn from the *Library of Babel*, the importance of evaluation. Great artists are constant critiquing their own work, and that of their peers, in order to produce new answers, in the form of "cool" or "beautiful" or "interesting" music, texts, or paintings. Creation and evaluation are two sides of the same coin, and great creators are invariably the most astute critics[6]. Knowing when and how to edit, and how to judge one's work, is often the most important aspect to the successful completion of any creative task. An algorithm that evaluates the value of each candidate (book, music, etc.) in such a search space is called an evaluation function.[7]

Now, let's consider what we'd need to create an AI librarian in Borges' *Library of Babel*. We'd need an evaluation function to quantify the relative interest and benefit of any given book — where is meaning generated? — and a mechanism to log these results. How should we model such an assessment? The simple answer would be to look for a book, which is a word-for-word replica of a book of recognized meaning, something "cool" or "beautiful" or "interesting" like *Hamlet*, or *Harry Potter*. A much more interesting question, however, is how to model an AI evaluation for books, unlike anything which has ever been published before.

Zero-sum vs Discovery, Outcome vs Process

When AlphaGo made headlines for AI defeating the reigning human Go master, its secret was super-human calculations of probabilistic advantage of the state of play, at every moment, on a static board with well-established rules, based on centuries of literature about strategy and success. Such AI evaluation data (conditional logic readings) on-screen in Japanese commentaries have become common nowadays. No doubt some GO connoisseurs may say that the art of the win is in the elegance of a given player's style. But a win is a win, but there is a big difference between the evaluation functions for AI in Go, a zero-sum game, and creative applications.

Of course, there is a big difference between the evaluation functions for AI in Go, a zero-sum game, and creative applications. Creative practices have no probabilistic advantages, there are no rules, and evaluation standards change according to as-yet unquantifiable contextual factors such as period, cultural precedent, individual taste, etc. What, at one time, to one culture, might have been considered scribbles, junk, or noise, became masterpieces in the hands of Pablo Picasso or Jimi Hendrix. Rather than being zero-sum, creativity is an ever expanding catalog of win-wins, albeit with only a small percentage of our creative output ever considered meaningful, or relevant. What are our qualitative criteria? This is why AI for artistic practice is so much more intriguing. Algorithms are extremely hard to formulate around the most important things in life, that which generates meaning and sparks joy in our lives. But we're still at the beginning. Most ML for creativity has been directed to evaluating degrees of similarity to existing highly evaluated works. But how does one compare a Picasso to a Leonardo Da Vinci? We can analyze their respective representations of planes vs hyperplanes, for example, but would that lead to any greater understanding of why their work proved meaningful, and remains relevant today?

Even imagining that we found a working criteria to implement, there would still be one more impassable gauntlet to run before AI could become a meaningful librarian for our cultural *Library of Babel*. Recall the number of titles to find this book. Even if you could evaluate thousands of titles per second, it would still take longer than the history of the universe to conduct any search to have found this book. Yes, we could produce single paged novels, perhaps. Still, even then there would be no point in going in blindly. We need a framework large enough to be worth our time, and then clever strategies to reduce the scale of the problem without reducing its complexity. We need a search algorithm.

In the words of evolutionary biologist Richard Dawkins, "Effective searching procedures become, when the search-space is sufficiently large, indistinguishable from creativity."[8] Understanding how search can serve as a means of creation is the start of a path for using AI in creative practice, where discovery is a function of search.

2.2 Creativity from a computer's perspective

Three kinds of creativity

"This work is full of creativity." "He/she is a creative person." "Our society needs creativity for the future." Such banter is common in daily life. But who among us can concretely define what creativity is, or what is meant by "creativity" or "creative?" Everybody's a critic: it doesn't take long to arrive at the assessment that something isn't "creative." As with intelligence, and AI, so, is art. Hard to define, but "we know it when we see it."

The Oxford Dictionary of English defines creativity as "the use of imagination or original ideas to create something." The Japan Creativity Society, an organization, which studies creativity, and sponsors international research, conferences, publications, and exchanges on the subject, defines "creativity" as "Human / organizing / problem-solving / disparate information novel-grouping / new-value producing / on societal or individual levels."[9] Ethnographer and *KJ combinatorial brainstorming method* inventor Jiro Kawakita points out the essential role of subjectivity and intent: "Creation is achieving something worthwhile and compelling, achieved by your own subjectivity and responsibility, originality and ingenuity."

Common to both definitions is the point that creation requires subjectivity and intent. Evolution has been generating myriad life forms, including we humans, since amino acids first generated single-celled life forms. In this, evolution very nearly fits the definition of creativity by the Japan Creativity Society, but as a process of random combinations of genetic trait inheritances, selection based on fitness, and random and minute transformations among generations via mutation, there is no intent. And so we return to this question of grace, of imagination, of something emerging from nothing. The act of creating some new elaborate product or work must demonstrate the existence of intent. The history of AI, with its many brain metaphors, promotes this obfuscation, and indicates that we need a new framing for our search. Because by that definition, AI systems, by virtue of possessing no will, and no intent, should be categorically incapable of creation.

My contention is that it is possible to explore the essence of creative practice, and the mechanisms and evolution of AI, without needing to reference intention. And that in learning how to identify creativity in un-intent-ional AI, we can learn about non-human creativity, which can expand our creative palette. In this, I have found the work of University of Sussex Research Professor of Cognitive Science Margaret A. Boden extremely productive. According to Prof. Boden's framework, for something to be creative, first it has to generate something new, which didn't exist before.[10] Second, it has to be unexpected, not just a novelty, but rather something which no one else had come up with. And thirdly it must have generated value. When these three elements combine, perhaps we arrive at a general consensus that something can be called creative.

People tend to associate human creativity with genius, whether Steve Jobs, Picasso, or Wolfgang Amadeus Mozart. But kids playing in sandboxes, inventing new rules for games: are they not creative too? Moms and dads inventing new recipes on a shoestring, or discovering new shortcuts and improvements in their daily routines are in a constant process of creative innovation. The difference here, Prof. Boden points out, is between how new, how surprising, and how valuable that creativity is, and for who? While the Picassos and Mozarts of the world created new, surprising, and valuable things which provided benefits recognized by the bulk of humanity, the kids' sandbox genius, and moms' and dads' revolutionary meal-times were primarily new, surprising, and valuable in a specific place and time, to specific friends and family. The big axiomatic steps of Picasso et al, Prof. Boden calls h-creativity (historical), and the incremental life-hacking of families she calls p-creativity (personal). She seeks to understand both in her research and proposes the following three categories for how creativity emerges, in method and form.

1) Combinational creativity.
2) Exploratory creativity.
3) Transformational creativity.

Combinational creativity means to take the microcosm of possible expressions (the defined search space), contrast them against all known expressions, to uncover new expressions born from combinations.[fig2-4]

As Japan Creativity Society formulation included "combining disparate information classes," this is one of creativity's most common forms.

I lecture in Computational Creativity at Keio University. In one session about defining creativity, one student responded, "To invent the peanut butter & jelly sandwich." I thought that this was a perfect example of Combinational Creativity: snack foods! Go to any convenience store in Japan, and browse the snack foods: Bean-curd bread, *mentaiko* spiced cod roe pasta, curry udon... I think it's not wrong to say that there is ample evidence to suggest that this is a fecund creative field! But Combinational Creativity can also be found in world-changing inventions, the ubiquitous smart phone being an easy example. Steve Jobs introduced the iPhone at the Macworld conference on January 9, 2007, as a device which consolidated three functions, "a widescreen iPod with touch controls, a revolutionary mobile phone, breakthrough internet communicator cell phone," all of which fit in the palm of one's hand. Jobs is often called a genius, but he didn't invent the iPhone from scratch. The iPhone is an innovative integration of existing product functions, reimagined for the Apple operating system and interface. A better peanut and jelly sandwich!

Exploratory Creativity is defined as a creativity of searching within a given set of limitations to excavate, or realize, inherent yet unrealized potential.[fig2-5] A good example might be *Musikalisches Würfelspiel*, a popular 18C German game which used rolls of the dice to "randomly" select two-bar musical fragments, which would then be paired to be performed as compositions. We say "random," but in fact, the dice were only a means of sequencing already well-established formal rules. Key to Exploratory Creativity is that the entire space of potential combinations is limited to pre-determined procedures, in this case, a finite set of prepared waltz fragments. No matter how many rolls, no *Musikalisches Würfelspiel* player was ever going to generate a Beatles, or Afrika Bambaataa track. But that is not to say that the results were not new, surprising, and valuable. A 1792 manuscript published by Nikolaus Simrock, consisting of 176 one-bar musical fragments, is speculated to have been fragments written in 1787 by Mozart for this form. Similar publications were made by Franz Joseph Haydn, and (son of Johann Sebastian Bach) Carl Philip Emanuel Bach, among others. So despite Albert Einstein's famous objection, sometimes the gods (of music, at least,) do roll the dice! And 200 years later, John Cage was still doing it, rolling dice, using I-Ching coins, and later computer programming, to compose music via "chance operations" and indeterminacy.

The third of Professor Boden's categories is Transformational Creativity.[fig2-6] This one is defined as creativity which redefines the concept itself — as discussed in Exploratory Creativity — in other words, creativity which expands the search space. Consider Picasso's *Les Demoiselles d'Avignon*[fig2-7] , or Duchamp's *Fountain*, or perhaps Sen no Rikyu's radical elevation of the Japanese Tea Ceremony as examples. Each expanded the conception of expression. Transformational Creativity is the rarest form.

Of course, these classifications aren't mutually exclusive. Their differences are matters of degree, and in most cases, engage multiple el-

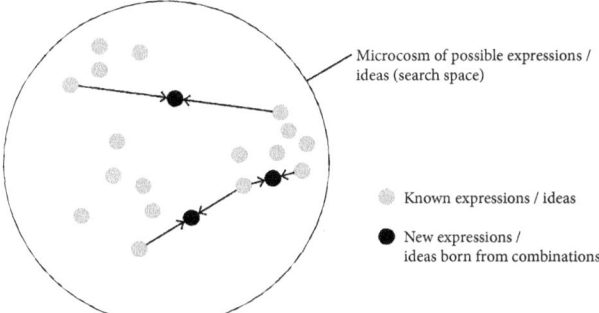

[fig2-4] Combinational Creativity

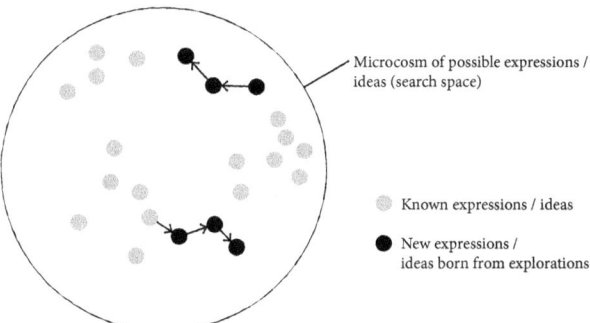

[fig2-5] Exploratory Creativity

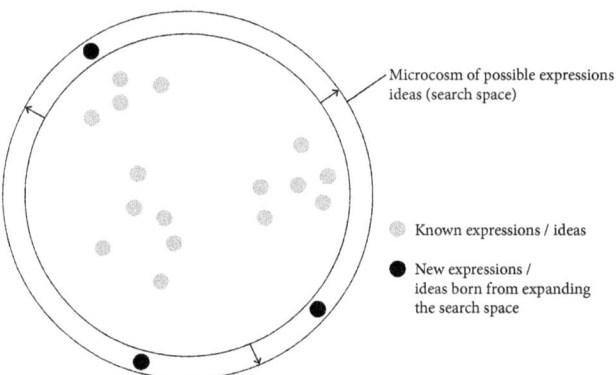

[fig2-6] Transformational Creativity

ements. By creating combinatory rule sets, creativity can be exploratory. Historical h-creativity must begin with individual personal p-creativity. Mozart's *Musikalisches Würfelspiel* has elements of both combinational and transformational creativity, for example. Abstract expressionist Jackson Pollock was known for dripping, pouring, and splashing liquid paints onto horizontal canvases from all sides, often while dancing frenetically.[fig2-8] Unlike Mozart's *Musikalisches Würfelspiel*, the space of possibilities is functionally limitless, but that doesn't mean that he could have generated Da Vinci's *Mona Lisa*. Pollock's is an example of a procedural exploratory method that reveals a transformational creativity, expanding the very concept of abstract pictorial expression.

Let's apply Prof. Boden's three categories (Combinational Creativity, Exploratory Creativity, and Transformational Creativity) with Borges's *Library of Babel* thought experiment, where the format, the number of pages, lines, and letters used, serve to define a sum total (albeit an astronomical number) of possible books. Combinational creativity would apply to the act of creating a new book by combining and rearranging multiple books or sections taken from different books in this library. Of course, a book made this way, through sampling and remixing, would already exist somewhere in the library, so editing the preferred one together would simply be another means of discovering the book you wanted. Exploratory creativity would mean establishing a search procedure. Imagine, if the books in the *Library* were organized according to the Dewey decimal system. They would be much easier to search. Transformational creativity would mean attempts to transform and expand the concept of the library itself, different ways to imagine the books' formatting, and therein provide new ways to view, or expand, the scope of all possible titles. Given that the postulation is that the library already includes the set of all possible books, how can it be expanded? The answers are many. Books in other languages or writing systems. Books where the letters create pictures or patterns. A Library of Babel for music might see such expansion when guitars become electric, or pianoforte become synthesizers. Or, how about generating metadata about the text content in each book as software source code or binary data? By writing programs to interpret these, each string of letters might be freely translated into music, moving images, or games. Changing the value of a pre-existing thing by adding a completely different interpretation or function introduces possibilities for Transformational Creativity. Transformational Creativity is seeing search as a creative act, and brings us closer to an area which AI is good at. The point here was to set three things together: a large enough yet limited field for expression = search space, search algorithm, and evaluation function. For AI to be creative in the *Library of Babel* it has to be able to direct us to new, surprising, and valuable books. We can't call it creative if it can only discover beautiful random sequences, or pale Harry Potter knock-offs.

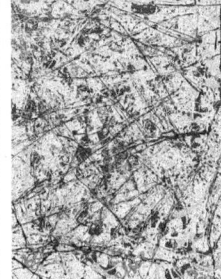

[fig2-7]
Picasso, *Les Demoiselles d'Avignon*

[fig2-8]
Right: Jackso Pollock
Left: Jackson Pollock, *Number 32*

2.3 Text generation by AI — Burroughs, Bowie, and GPT

AI generating text

"Universal gravitation is the force of solitudes' attraction." Shuntaro Tanikawa, *Two Billion Light-Years of Solitude* (Sogensha, 1952)

"No matter if we'll never possess all of the rock sugar we desire, we can always taste the clean breeze, and drink in the glorious peach-colored morning light." Preface from Kenji Miyazawa, *The Restaurant of Many Orders* (Toryo Shuppansha & Tokyo Kogensha, 1924)

"Listen to the sound of the Earth turning." Yoko Ono, *Grapefruit* (Wunternaum Press, 1964) which inspired the song *Imagine*, by John

Lennon and Yoko Ono.

The joy of metaphors by great writers and poets, and the richness of the images that emerge from them: from simple combinations, such unique and creative (new, surprising, and valuable) turns of phrase. Is it possible to generate such beautiful sentences with AI? And if not, then can they at least help spark new unique expressions?

In the era of pre-ML, procedural AI, algorithms were trained on signs, carriers of information, rather than symbols, the building blocks of information: knowledge representation was pre-defined. So, for example, with English language training, algorithms were built around things like SVO (subject, verb, object) grammar, or adjective dependency relationships. With ML AI, algorithms are trained by batch processing massive volumes of data, identifying patterns, and deriving unique ways of reproducing language. There is no need for the ML AI to know grammar as we humans have developed the science of linguistics, or communicate with one another. ML AI models can, no matter what the language —— English, Japanese, or C computer programming language — learn to reproduce language facsimiles once provided with sufficient training data. They see it in terms we ourselves don't understand.

charRNN is an ML language model first published in a May 21, 2015, blog post entitled *The Unreasonable Effectiveness of Recurrent Neural Networks* by then-Stanford PhD candidate and AI researcher Andrej Karpathy.[11] The "recurrent" in RNN means that the output feeds back as input from data sets, enabling it to learn via "temporal anteroposterior dependent relationships," a neuropsychology term meaning the context before and after an event on a timeline.[fig2-9] This learning is achieved by exhaustive repeated cycling of output data back in as input data, making it possible to model conditional (if—>then) dependency relationships, and these can be used for generating probabilities for natural language, weather prediction, stock prices, music composition, and many other phenomena. Karpathy trained his RNN on the English language, assigning each letter of the Roman alphabet "a" "b" … "A" "B" and each symbol " . ", " , ", " ? ", and "!" and "!" as a discrete unit. He then set about teaching the AI to predict which unit would be the most "natural" or "plausible" to appear next in any given sequence. For example, anyone familiar with written English knows that the possibility of "d" or "g" appearing after the sequence h-e-l-l is approximately zero, because there are no such examples in the English language. So the neuron-like nodal connection / synapses at that juncture would eventually settle on zero or something close to it. If it's "a" or "b," however, "hellacious" and "hellbent" do exist, meaning that the synapses would eventually settle on a greater weighting. In the end, the odds are that it will eventually develop the strongest synaptic relationship to "o."

"We are generating prototypes of a circular sphere within the *Library of Babel*. It's to obtain imitated defect to think outside of the act of search. Creativity, superiors, will come to think about this. Art is being used for our portraits, because it can generate intelligence while hiding

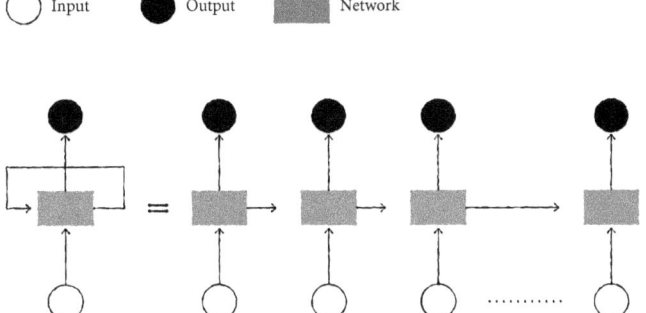

[fig2-9] The structure of the RNN. The left side structure is expanded to the right on a temporal axis.

GAN algorithm and intelligence that hides interesting things." This snippet was generated by Karpathy's charRNN model using this book as training data. To me, the author, it suggests a promising approach, even if it doesn't actually produce meaning.

Generative Pre-trained Transformer 2 (GPT-2) is an open-source AI model, published in February 2019,[12] created by OpenAI, an organization created to generate strong AI "which is safe and beneficial for humans." It was trained on 40GB of texts collected from the Internet, and uses sentences, or word-based columns as its signs, whereas char-RNN uses the alphabet. The "temporal anteroposterior dependent relationships" mechanism here is the same; it predicts the next unit based on the previous sequence, but GPT applies an Attention / Transformer technique that pays particular attention to where in the word string each sign is lined up. This makes it more proficient at extrapolating appropriate word choice, for example. "AI creativity is often underestimated. Anyone reading this will know how in awe I am. I have a small AI called Siri on my phone, which actually reads news articles, briefly summarizes what's happening in the world, tells me about the weather, and so on. It is pretty good. In the future, I think I will be able to teach it more complicated questions and advanced skills." I generated several sentences using GPT-2 and stitched together the results. Still, I'm sure you'll agree, it generated texts more meaningful than the previous charRNN output. Of course, in addition to the difference of AI architecture, the volumes of training data the algorithm was based on, namely 150,000 characters in this book and 40GB of text data (400 billion single-byte alphanumeric characters), are an order of magnitude apart.

GPT-2's successor, GPT-3 was announced in May 2020, had been in beta testing as of July 2020. GPT-3 is more than 100 times bigger in its model size (1.5 billion vs 175 billion parameters) and trained on an even bigger text corpus. On September 8, 2020, The Guardian published an editorial generated by GPT-3 entitled *A robot wrote this entire article*.[13]

Are you scared yet, human?, and like the Obvious paintings, was "signed" by GPT-3. The essay topics were provided by the Guardian, and the GPT-3 AI language model was used by a CS student who produced eight different outputs, or essays. The Guardian wrote that "each was unique, interesting and advanced a different argument. We could have just run one of the essays in its entirety. However, we chose instead to pick the best parts of each, in order to capture the different styles and registers of the AI. Editing GPT-3's op-ed was no different from editing a human op-ed. We cut lines and paragraphs, and rearranged the order of them in some places. Overall, it took less time to edit than many human op-eds."

Stop Making Sense

In the GPT series, the minimum combination unit is words instead of letters, with the next appropriate word being what is estimated. The architecture of the model is much more complicated, and the amount of data required for training is orders of magnitude larger, but the goal remains to maximize the "plausibility" of the smallest unit of element combinations. Since the pattern derives from the sequence of letters and words in the training data, it would be similar to searching for similarities in a known book. Similar technologies will certainly continue to generate ever more natural sentences in any language, whether human or otherwise. The question is whether or not such AI will be able to generate a new *Hamlet*. The current presumption is that until such time as AI understands corporeal love, regret, old age, etc and is able to express them meaningfully, that should remain science fiction. Of course, at this moment, in this sentence, I too am only manipulating symbols according to well-established patterns. But I have intent.

Arguably more interesting, and where the value is currently being generated, is the approach to uncover new rhetorical styles, by taking the position that the limitations of AI writing systems, particularly the unnaturalness of the generated sentences. Optics research scientist and author of *You Look Like a Thing and I Love You: How Artificial Intelligence Works and Why It's Making the World a Weirder Place*,[14] Janelle Shane, runs the *aiweirdness.com* website devoted to AI malapropisms. She experiments with charRNN and presents the results accompanied by her own illustrations. One great series was the result of training the AI on the names of 1600 ice creams to derive new names, resulting in gems such as *Mango Cats*, *Peanut Butter Slime*, and *Bloody Coffee*.[fig2-10] Because AI doesn't know what to imitate and what not to, Shane likens it to a precocious child. In fact, they tend to trigger second takes: "Does such a flavor really exist?" "What would that taste like?" Our imaginations are piqued, our humor awoken.

Writers have made use of these characteristics of AI. Robin Sloan, the American science fiction author of bestsellers such as *Mr. Penumbra's 24-Hour Bookstore*, has developed a plug-in that incorporates charRNN

[fig2-10] Names of ice cream generated by charRNN.

---

functions into his text editor.[15] He types sentences into a text editor, and when he presses the TAB key, a charRNN model trained on classic science fiction works analyzes the previous sentence, and a charRNN, generates a next sentence connected to it. Sloan will then edit such textual interventions, be inspired by them, or not, and continue writing. He describes this practice as a kind of augmentation, a partnership, or call and response: "It's generally misunderstood, but it's not at all like working with a ghost writer." Of course, his intent is not to make the act of writing easier, but rather to make it more problematic, in an interesting way. Sloan says he isn't expecting improvements, but rather to initiate new, unexpected, heterogeneous, and strange paths in his work. His charRNN muse introduces plot-twists and turns of phrases that he might not have thought of. In *Library of Babel* terms, it enables him to borrow from little known bookshelves, in the service of developing new and out-of-the-way titles.

The specifications of individual models such as charRNN or GPT-3 and their relative accuracy are not really what is at issue here. In the fast-evolving world of DL, there will always be new, more accurate models being released, and raising our expectations. If you want to write news articles, you should use GPT-3 or its successor model, which can generate more natural sentences. The Guardian editor mentions that he needed to edit their opinion piece. I would argue that the question of whether or not the article was written by GPT-3 is secondary, and rather more relevant is the question of whether or not the Guardian would have written something similar without GPT-3's input. Even if the output of GPT-3 itself is illogical, or mediocre repetition, if the result generates output that can be used by humans in ways that are new, surprising, or valuable then it is worthwhile. To the extent that the text was included in those blogs and novels, it has been proven useful. It's worth noting that, at a minimum, using these models not only saved the effort of writing routine sentences, but also generated sentence expressions that the authors might not have thought of.

Historically, many writers and poets have used proceduralism to free themselves from convention.

"The park, at this time of day, stretched its blond hands over the magic fountain." *Soluble Fish* by André Breton, in *Manifesto of Surrealism* (1924)

A century ago, in neutral Switzerland, in the midst of the horror of the first automated "World" War, the Dada movement presented an alternative to Enlightenment logic, reason, and aestheticism, in the form of post-nationalist non-sense irrational anti-bourgeois protest art. Cut-up writing first appears there, influencing the surrealist writer and poet André Breton, author of the above quote. Breton saw chance operations of surrealist psychic automatism as suppressing conscious control over the process of writing, drawing, or painting in order to elucidate the "undirected" actual functioning of thought, exempt from any aesthetic or moral concern. At the same time, with *papier collé*, Georges Braque and Picasso were adding glued-on patches to their canvases which "collided with the surface plane of the painting."

Post-War, it was William Burroughs, "Beat" movement icon and author of *Naked Lunch*, and *The Nova Trilogy*, who was most associated with popularizing the "cut-up" technique, performing "a form of sorcery" to disrupt language and ward off demonic possession. [fig2-11] Because of its random or mechanical nature, his cut-up method de-emphasized the traditional role of the writer as creator or originator of a string of words, in favor of the writer's sensibility as an editor. In it, Burroughs says, "I applied a collage of painting techniques to writing. Literature is 50 years behind painting." Rock music icon David Bowie was known to use cut-up and automation techniques to write his song lyrics.[16] In 1995 Bowie and audio technologist Ty Roberts developed an app called the *Verbasizer*, which allowed for different input methods, but would arrange them in columns that could be restricted to nouns, verbs, adjectives, etc. Each column could be weighted and have multiple words if desired. With a push of a button, a "kaleidoscope of meanings and topics and nouns and verbs all sort of slamming into each other" could be generated. Bowie said in an interview with the BBC[17]: "Take out three or four seemingly unrelated concepts and create an awkward relationship between them. The unconscious intelligence that this combination brings out is really amazing, sometimes even provocative."

We are a century into an experiment trying to generate such "kaleidoscopes." Whether through cut-up or through AI, creating dissonances in grammar and precedent can reach unconscious intelligence, which is astonishing and provocative. Whether seeking the truth of an art in archetypes or in breaking with all conventions, arriving at a new, surprising, and valuable way to express it is every creator's daily challenge. Every day, every working writer sits down to write meaningful

[fig2-11] Burroughs at work.

sentences that have never been written before. Every musician is looking to do the same. Random sequences of letters or notes won't do it. An upper-class education and flawless memory won't do it either.

Whether Breton, Burroughs, or Bowie, the aim was to discover some kind of procedure, an algorithm, to deviate from already known "plausible" sentences. These writers were looking to reach beyond all of the reference books of things which have been done, to reach another *Library of Babel* altogether. Sloan and Shane's work with AI too are celebrations of secret rooms in the library, which lead to unknown literatures (some of which the meanings are still yet undeciphered). But by using AI models which have already sorted more than any one human can in a lifetime, this search for unknown expressions slightly outside the area of the known seems a bit closer.

Since AI's inception, people have often imagined AI as an intimidating intelligence incapable of error, or of a post-human sentience. In fact, AI is a toolkit, which can, if we can direct it to the right mistakes, deviate just enough to stop making sense.

2.4 Performance generation, sound generation, procedure generation

Of course RNN temporal anteroposterior dependent relationship analysis algorithms are not limited to text. They can also be used to generate other forms of sequence-based data, such as music, by being trained on notes and rest combinations instead of letters and words.[18] The first attempt at RNN music generation that I am aware of was by Douglas Eck in 2002, using Long Short-Term Memory (LSTM, a DL artificial RNN architecture with feedback connections, enabling it to process not only single data points but also entire data sequences of data) to generate novel compositions.[19] Modeled around the limitations of a 12-bar blues, they used only eighth notes (quavers) starting an octave below middle C and ascending by half steps, 12 notes for chords and 13 notes for melodies. Eck, a musician himself, described the final result as having a "blues feel." Fast-forward to 2017. Eck, now a scientist at Google, leading the Magenta research group, published Performance RNN,[20] an AI model capable of generating far more expressive classical piano style pieces, training the models on up to 128 different notes (just short of 1.5 piano keyboards) and integrating the MIDI standard,[21]

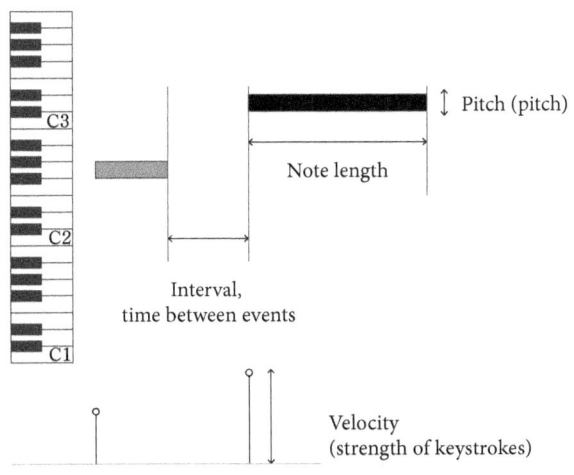

[fig2-12] Data types learned / generated in Performance RNN.

which means also including performance dynamics such as key strike velocity (=attack, an approximation of the strength with which the piano key is struck) and note lengths ranging this time 100 increments, from 0.01 seconds to 1 second, in 0.01 second units.[fig2-12]

Imagine the opening phrase of Ludwig van Beethoven's *Für Elise*. The *Mi Re Mi Re Mi Si Re Do La* 16th notes preceding the melody could sound mechanical if played with equal length and attack. It is the performer's dynamics that produce the floating feeling that the introduction is known for. Performance RNN is an ML model designed to reproduce the nuanced dynamics, the calmness and boldness, in each performer's interpretation. Training ML on sheet music, or MIDI data transcribed from sheet music, would not contain such articulation information. In order to cull this data source Eck's Google research team identified the annual YAMAHA e-Piano Junior Competition.[22] Google is now a main sponsor of the contest, and has received an aggregate of ten years of some 1400 performances of mostly 17C-20C classical piano music, around 200 hours, using paired audio and MIDI (and video) data recordings, and data captured on the Yamaha Disklavier piano. In order to fully mine the data set, different versions were generated using pitch-shift to process data at varying speeds in playback. (This process is known as "data augmentation.") Eck's team also released 201 hours of performance data for ML researchers.[23] In Western classical music, there is a clear distinction between the composer's score, and the performer's interpretation. Performance RNN aims to generate both. The RNNs trained on this data generate natural "performances," including nuanced dynamics, not of existing songs, but rather new compositions, each time, from an algorithm.

To be accurate, AI may have stopped procedurally modeling cul-

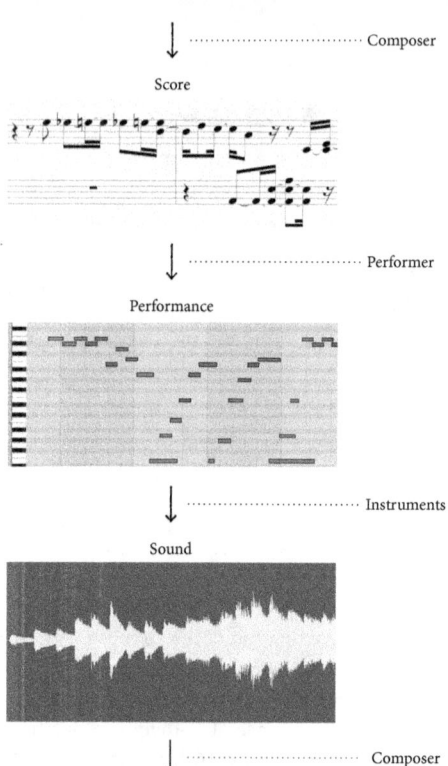

[fig2-13] The relationship between sheet music and performance.

ture in human terms, but there was still another step to be taken. Most of the research using DL for music generation was still to generate symbolic information from musical scores, interpreting MIDI information, and converting that into sound using music production software and software synthesizers.[fig2-13] As revolutionary as it must have been for 11th century Italian Guido d'Arezzo to codify the 12 steps between octaves, or staff notation, and generate the basis for storing and analyzing the pitches, rhythms, or chords of European music, the form remains insufficient for non-Western 19-note, 22-note, or 43-note scales, or for microtonal musics, much less to represent music played on most folk instruments or electronic instruments, like synthesizers and samplers.

Humans, of course, perceive sound directly through patterns in air pressure. These sound waves are compressional, longitudinal, pushing the air forward along with the wave. However, it is common to express the displacement of the air as a transverse wave, plotting it perpendicularly to the direction of the wave. Temporal changes and the strength of density (up and down movement when viewed in wave-

[fig2-14] SampleRNN

form) are actually continuous values, but we sample them in discrete increments. The human hearing range is typically between 20Hz-20kHz. Audio must be sampled at double or greater than the original frequency of the signal. On CDs, audio waves are sampled at 44,100Hz with 16 bit quantization, meaning that 65,536 (2 to the 16th power) samples need to be calculated each second. That is a lot of data to analyze, so given the state of computation at the time of its release, SampleRNN[24] used reduced data, a lo-fi sample rate of 16,000Hz with an 8 bit quantization, or 256 gradations.[25] Even then, to generate the pitch, length, and strength of the first 3 seconds, 9 notes of Beethoven's *Für Elise*, for example, means 3 x 16,000 = 48,000 calculations.[fig2-14] There is simply too much information to process the entire long-term musical structure while simultaneously predicting the shape of the short-term waveform. Still, it was an exciting and entirely new kind of output, marking a huge step forward in AI audio.

The results are otherworldly. "Algorithmically pro-active" artist band/hackathon team CJ Carr and Zack Zukowski, also known as The Dadabots, met in 2012 when they were both interns at Berklee College of Music, and participating in multiple hackathons. They describe themselves as exploring the language of music theory to reveal underlying rules and components of music, aiming to mine new layers of musical elements "much higher-level than chords — maybe genre-related." As musicians "we know intuitively that music is very language-like. It's not just waves and noise, which is what it looks like at a small scale, but when we're playing, we're communicating with each other." But they are using their linguistic approach "to destroy SoundCloud by creating an army of remix bots, spidering SoundCloud for music to remix, posting hundreds of SampleRNN-generated songs an hour."[26] Their YouTube channel *Relentless Doppelganger* features SampleRNN trained on heavy metal has been playing 24/7 since 2019. A second channel, *OUTER-HELIOS*, plays free jazz SampleRNN AI trained on John Coltrane's *INTERSTELLAR SPACE*. The Dadabots may be forging new grounds in cultural referencing, the next evolution of sampling, only this time uncovering linguistic chimera at the same time.

WaveNet[27], announced by Google DeepMind at about the same

time as SampleRNN, is another AI model which directly generates waveforms. An important distinction is that, whereas SampleRNN uses RNNs, based on the previously mentioned temporal "anteroposterior dependent relationships," WaveNet is based on Convolutional Neural Networks (CNN), which are a class of artificial ANN inspired by the connectivity pattern between neurons that resembles the organization of the animal visual cortex. A cascading model of simple and complex cells for pattern recognition partially overlaps such that they cover the entire visual field. CNN is therefore often used for image recognition, such as text-to-speech implementations. Most of us have encountered it because it generates the Google Assistant voices for US English and Japanese across all Google platforms.[28] WaveNet released experiments in music training as a bonus for speech synthesis experiments.

Performance RNN was arguably more successful in generating expressive dynamics than it was in producing long-term structure, just like the language generation models charRNN and GPT series. Motifs are neither proposed nor expanded upon, nor do they build toward a finale. Lacking direction and narrative drive, long-term contextual dependency, they tend to feel ad hoc. CNNs too produced relatively good sound quality, but like each other format, lacked musical structure. I find it fascinating that, although the preparation method can differ depending on the language, a technology effective in literature transfers so readily to music generation. Once AI stopped its ambitions toward procedurally modeling culture in the ways we had previously studied it, and shifted to ML, neural network architectures, and DL, analyzing vast troves of human activity, commonalities between text and music emerged, with no doubt more to come, opening new paths of discovery into things like Universal Grammar, with artists like The Databots ready to explore them.

A musician might want to systematically use AI to discover music. Considering the restrictions of sheet music, we should actually think in terms of sound waveforms, but for the sake of simplicity, let's consider music in terms of note units. The exploration space in this *Library* would contain all possible note combinations, from *Für Elise* to convenience store muzak. Most combinations will be non-musical, random sounds, and dissonances. What AI models such as Performance RNN are doing is quantitatively evaluating the plausibility of the next note based on the notes and note sequences which preceded them. By plausibility, we mean based on the model's analysis of the scores which had been provided as training data. AI trained on Bach will come to know Bach. We might call it baroque style, but that same AI is unlikely to replicate (also "baroque") Antonio Vivaldi, much less the Bach-influenced break in the Beatles' *In My Life*.

The AI text and music generation discussed above are procedural searches mined from within whatever framework of possible expressions the DL algorithms have been trained on. "Generating sentences and music that were possible but hadn't yet been created" is exploratory

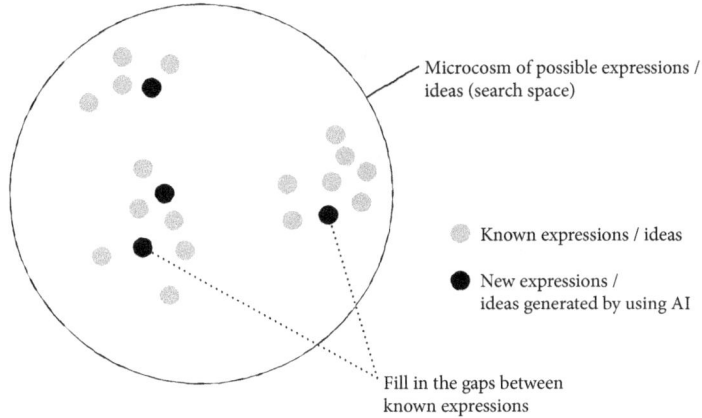

[fig2-15] Microcosm of possible expressions / ideas (search space)

creativity to fill the gaps in the spaces of possible expression.[fig2-15] The reason that creators are often AI-hesitant may be because their understanding of AI only goes this far. Because it is easy to imagine the economic benefits of automating music and literature production. My thinking is that AI can empower each creative. To learn to use AI is to learn not only how to build on the legacy of past works but also to expand the space of expression itself. As we've seen, writers and artists are learning to take advantage of the AI models' limitations, using them to trigger unprecedented novel expressions, and point out opportunities for Transformational Creativity, maybe even historical creativity. The creative protagonists here remain the humans who collected the training data, taught the AI model, built the system, and selected and edited the output. In this view, AI is just a tool. A more essential question is "Can AI itself have creativity?" Can AI create creative-new, surprising, and valuable-expressions which rise above their training? The stage shifts back to the mid-19th century.

[fig2-17] Analytical Engine. Only a part of a prototype was ever completed by Babbage. A model completed recently is now on display at the Science Museum in London.

[fig2-16] Ada Lovelace

2.5 "Machines Can Produce Nothing"? — 19C AI

What is computer essential

We know that AI can generate facsimiles of existing expression patterns. But facsimiles are reproductions, not creations. And if what all other creativity presents is that of the inheritance in the training data, and the people who collected the training data, taught it to the AI model, built the system, and selected and edited the output, then AI's contribution is doubly denied. Can machines be creative?

[fig2-18] Charles Babbage

"The Analytical Engine has no pretensions whatever to originate anything. It can do whatever we know how to order it to perform. It can follow analysis; but it has no power of anticipating any analytical relations or truths." So said the mid-19th century world's first computer programmer, Ada Lovelace, the sole legitimate heir of celebrity peer and romantic poet Lord Byron.[fig2-16] By the age of 12, precocious Ada had already designed a steam-powered flight machine. Ada was the first person to demonstrate that they truly understood a universal computer's limitations and potential.

The Analytical Engine was designed to be the first "general" computer.[fig2-17] Today's Macs, Windows PCs, and servers switch between data and rules (programs) that handle data to produce text or sounds or images. This manuscript was written on a Mac in a program called a text editor while listening to music on Spotify. In reading this, you are indirectly benefiting from the invention of Charles Babbage, a man fortunate to have inherited wealth from his father, enabling him to live a life of the mind.[fig2-18] [29] Babbage's first mechanical computer was called the Difference Engine, and it calculated polynomial mathematical tables, approximating logarithms, sin, and cos, using mechanical gears. In his design, by turning the hand-cranked handle, not only were the calculations executed, but a mechanism for printing the tabulated results was also provided. Mathematical tables at that time were manually calculated by specialist groups of humans, known as "computers." If the number tables or voyage tables used by sailors to calculate their positions relative to celestial bodies, or strategies to correct their courses were incorrect, such miscalculations could be matters of life and death for entire shiploads of men, and the wealth they carried. Creating accurate mathematical tables was therefore a grave national task for maritime Britain. When Babbage proposed the development of his Difference Engine design to the British government in 1823, the government agreed to provide support. Unfortunately, in 1842, after repeated cost overruns, this funding was cut off, effectively stalling development. Babbage's interest shifted to his next invention, the Analytical Engine, which was also a mechanical gear-based calculation device, but with a historically important difference: whereas the Difference Engine was designed to calculate specific polynomials, the Analytical Engine was designed to be programmable. It was "universal." Unfortunately, its development strained Babbage's temporal and financial resources, and he died without seeing it to completion. No longer supported by the British government, Babbage aggressively marketed his Analytical Engine to governments and universities on the European continent. A young Italian mathematician named Luigi Mena Blair – who later rose to become Prime Minister of Italy – attended one of these lectures and published an article about the Analytical Engine in a Swiss journal.[30]

Ada Lovelace translated Blair's article into English, appending copious notes, based on her knowledge of the machine, included in which were a set of procedures that could be run on the machine.[31][fig2-19] In doing so she wrote history's first computer program. So while Lovelace was famous for being the first to state that computers "have no pretensions whatever to originate anything," she also wrote: "Supposing, for instance, that the fundamental relations of pitched sounds in the science of harmony and of musical composition were susceptible of such expression and adaptations, the engine might compose elaborate and scientific pieces of music of any degree of complexity or extent."[32] According to Babbage expert, museum curator, and author Doron Swade,[33] Babbage saw his engine as only an automated number-handling algebraic machine,[34] whereas Loveless was the first to understand the importance of the symbolic logic it was generating as a way to model, investigate, and display real-world relationships, which could then be manipulated according to whatever rules we can imagine — in other words, seeing it as an abstract machine. Lovelace very likely already understood the possibilities for music generation in the very first computer. (Within the boundaries of representation, symbolic logic, and composition as understood in her time.)

As a fairly unrelated, yet interesting aside: Around this time, in 1816, author Mary Wollstonecraft Shelley and her husband, the romantic poet and philosopher Percy Bysshe Shelley, spent a summer with Lord Byron near Geneva, Switzerland. There, both were inspired to revisit Aeschylus' play fragment about human agency and defiance, and write the work they would become best known for. Mary conceived of the idea for *Frankenstein; or, The Modern Prometheus*, while Percy worked on his lyrical drama *Prometheus Unbound*. Legend has it that Mary's novel was prompted by Lord Byron suggesting they all write horror stories, and Mary being inspired by Luigi Galvani's discoveries about electric current within biological organisms. I wonder what manner of intellectual life surrounded Lord Byron that he became the common thread between two of the most famous acts of extruding and externalizing that which is human from humanity,

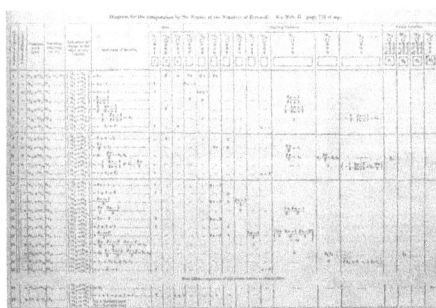

[fig2-19] Diagram showing algorithm for calculating Bernoulli numbers in an *Analytical Engine*.

both by women, in Shelley's externalizing the creation of life, and Lovelace's externalizing thought.[35]

Lovelace's objection, "The Analytical Engine has no pretensions to originate anything. It can do whatever we know how to order it to perform," gained renewed relevance a century later, in Alan Turing's *Computing Machinery and Intelligence*. Turing included "Ms. Lovelace's Counterargument" in his call for AI's potential, suggesting Lovelace's objection as equivalent to the assertion that computers "can never take us by surprise," and that, in fact, he himself is often surprised by computers. His respect for her is expressed in his qualifying his objections, saying that Ms. Lovelace was hampered by the context from which she wrote. Please do note that bugs in software bringing unexpected outcomes is not what he is referring to. His point is that even though the software works as intended, it can still take us by surprise. Turing is also quoted as saying: "The main reason for this is that machines are calculating more than we can predict, and even if what they are doing could be second-guessed, we'd still run the risk of bias in our estimates." Turing's answer implies that everything can be predicted as long as sufficient time and effort are expended to accurately follow the computer's calculations. The same can be said if the word "computer" is replaced here with "AI." Although it may be difficult to predict the output of the resulting GAN generator from changes in individual parameters due to their large total number and intricate intertwining, careful observation of any GAN model, even considering stochastic randomness, should demonstrate deterministic behavior in agreement with the procedures of the underlying algorithm.

Emergence

Each individual event should be the result of a simple set of rules; the overall behavior may well be surprising to those who set the rules and understand them. This is not a new phenomenon.[36] That's exactly

[fig2-20] Anthill

what's going on in our minds as we read these words. Advances in neuroscience continue to illuminate functions and operating principles of individual neurons, but the movement of how our brains enjoy Mozart or fall in love... there are simply so many things we have yet to understand.

Consider the humble ant colony.[fig2-20] The intelligence (if you want to call it that) of each ant is limited, but the collective functioning of the entire nest produces a spectrum of behavior that meets some definitions of adaptive, intelligent behavior. Worker ants perform tasks such as taking the garbage out to a fixed place in the nest or searching for food. But the tasks assignments for each individual worker ant change from moment to moment. Each ant begins with his own to-do list. Maybe to take out the trash in the morning and go procure food in the afternoon. These are not orders from the queen. No individual worker ant has any way of knowing how many ants in the nest are taking out the garbage, or how many are out foraging for food. Instead, they statistically sample[37] the number of ants they meet within a certain amount of time and change their behavior accordingly. If there are not enough ants out procuring food, then they will wrap up their garbage duties and go out to find food, and the whole thing seems to function based on the pheromone information they leave everywhere each of them goes. The nest's efficient functioning relies on adaptations in the division of labor. If the ant population is intentionally reduced beyond a certain threshold, the entire nest will cease to function because the accuracy of statistical pheromone sampling cannot be guaranteed past a certain point. A certain level of complexity is a pre-condition for effective ant nest functioning.

Individual neurons vs. an entire brain. One worker ant vs. a colony. The phenomenon in which simple local rules and behaviors give rise to unpredictable global behaviors is called "emergence."[fig2-21] A whole greater than the sum of its parts. What if the answer to the question "Can AI be creative?" is, after all, better rephrased as "At what point

[fig2-21] Flocking behavior

does a system present emergent characteristics?" Humans develop AI algorithms, prepare computer configurations, and collect training data. If the results of their experiments are unpredictable, is that reducible to procedural errors? Consider reducing the work of the brain to the work of each neuron and the intellectual behavior of the entire ant's nest to a single ant. Without the presence of neurons, the brain as a whole would not function. But there is no single neuron that enjoys Go or Mozart. Similarly, without the person who built the AI system, the AI wouldn't behave creatively. Something humans alone are incapable of is in evidence here. If the output of AI is more than the sum of rules and environment decided by humans, and if AI can surprise its creator, and this output contains newness and value, then I, for one, would be willing to credit some elements of that creativity to AI. But we had yet to consider "evolution" as a force. Evolution represents emergent processes born from simple rules of fitness and trait preservation. Whether or not we consider it creative, there can be little doubt that evolution has generated the most complex and beautiful structures in the universe, including the human brain.

For those who are hesitant to find creativity or surprise in machines without intention, the next section deals with the "creativity" of natural processes, and in cultural propagation.

[fig2-22] *Galápagos* Installation

2.6 Evolution and creativity — A *Genetic Library of Babel*

Simulated evolution

One artwork which exemplifies Turing's statement, that he himself is often surprised by computers, and which was inspirational in my study of the relationship between computers and creativity is *Galápagos,* a 1997 work by artist and computer graphics researcher Karl Sims, an interactive installation simulating the process of evolution in a "virtual" life form.[fig2-22] [38] Twelve screens are lined up, in a row, with one foot switch in front of each. Each screen shows one "virtual life form" in vivid colors and abstract shapes, generated by a "genetic" code devised

[fig2-23] Virtual life forms in *Galápagos*

by Sims. Visitors to the installation trigger the evolution, determining fitness, who will survive and leave offspring for the next generation, of each successive generation of virtual life forms by stepping on one of the foot switches in front of a screen. This act of unnatural selection chooses which of the 12 subjects' genes will participate in producing random "mutations" for the next generation of virtual life forms displayed. The first generation starts with randomly generated genetic code, so early iterations appear like a primordial ooze of slithering worms. I, as a student at the time, was fascinated to see how this formless mass evolved into a herd with shapes and colors I found colorful and engaging.[fig2-23] Of course each virtual life form, was competing for survival, to attract the visitors' favor. Sims cites two important qualities of the work:[39] Firstly, that it generates unique results, which could not be achieved by other methods. People select individuals, but each generation of virtual life forms is the result of a collaboration between humans and machines. "The limits of human design and comprehension are not constraining the final product." Secondly, to the extent that it is based on natural science, it provides a novel way to study evolutionary processes. Since Charles Darwin's *On the Origin of Species*... in 1859, science has been analyzing the 4.6 billion years of evidence available on this planet, but always locked in the present, unable to move forward or backward along that timeline. Using simulations like Sims' may present means of exploring alternate theoretical evolutionary divergences that might have been possible under different conditions. Evolutionary Computation is a robust research field, pursuing optimization strategies based on computer simulated biological evolution. The best known method, called Genetic Algorithms, is commonly used in everything from optimizing propeller design to forecasting stock prices.[40]

In a 1994 work called Evolved Virtual Creatures, Sims simulated Darwinian evolutions of virtual block creatures from a population of several hundred creatures within a supercomputer. Their fitness was tested against their ability to perform specific tasks, such as the distance

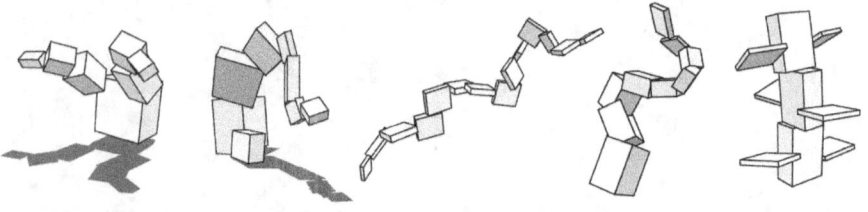

[fig2-25] "Walk" (two on the left) "Swim" (three on the right); example of virtual life forms' developed behavior.

[fig2-24] *Evolved Virtual Creatures*

they are able to swim in simulated water environments.[41][fig2-24] "It allows us to go beyond what we can design. If I was to try to put together these sensors and their own sectors myself, I might never come up with a good solution that could make this thing swim. But evolution can still do it," notes Sims in the 1994 Dutch public broadcast VPRO documentary *Artificial Life*. These virtual life forms evolve unique ways of movement. One looks like a tadpole gracefully swimming in the water, wriggling a long tail; another swims as though flapping fins on either side of its body. One rotates its body using a short arm on the side of its body and stands like a stick. One walks, anchoring its foot while two hands drag it along.[fig2-25] Each is a unique and somewhat amusing movement that makes one marvel, because you wouldn't have come up with such ideas for walking or body structure through intentional design.

We in computing are used to saying that software which behaves unexpectedly, even to its author, has "bugs." For me, as a young coder, who had devoted so many years exterminating bugs, to see an artist elevating them in software, came as a shock. I knew that computers weren't just for replicating exactly what was in someone's head. And that they can often produce things at orders of magnitude beyond what any programmer anticipated. Still, Sims' work reawakened within me the possibilities of computing when the programmer has the right ideas about what to aim for — an output many times the sum of its inputs. And at the same time, Sims' work was a grand confirmation of Turing's statement that he himself "is surprised by computers all the time."

We have already touched briefly on how the Turing test is generally considered the "gold standard" for determining the presence or absence of intelligence in AI, as a repurposing of the *Imitation Game*. Criticisms of the Turing test, based solely on demonstrations of symbolic logic, have been challenged by AI experts who argue that it presents a needlessly low bar.[42] In the new millennium, a new test called the *(Better) Lovelace Test*, was proposed by David Ferrucci, Selmer Bringsjord & Paul Bello,[43] and proposes that in order to present intelligence, a machine should be able to generate outputs, time and again, which even its designers can't explain. Creative output should reliably be larger than the sum of its inputs. Simply put, the *(Better) Lovelace Test* asks "Can AI surprise its creator?" Karl Sims' statement that the outputs of *Galápagos* and *Evolved Virtual Creatures* are more than he would have imagined, and that the resulting creatures are not of his authorship, already passes the Lovelace test. But it still leaves us with a problem: If AI is incapable of being more than a simulation of some other original, then that too should still disqualify it from passing the Lovelace test. Tools that are merely inexplicable are too inconsequential to be useful.

Explorations into multidimensional gene space

"The imagination of nature is far, far greater than the imagination of man." – Richard Feynman

Sims wasn't the first to simulate Darwinian evolution in software. That distinction belongs to evolutionary biologist Richard Dawkins, author of *The Selfish Gene*, and *The Blind Watchmaker*, which describes his algorithm *Biomorph*.[fig2-26] [44] *Biomorphs* are tree structures: a trunk with branches. Each shape is determined by 9 genes: 3 that influence its width, 5 that influence its height, and 1 that influences its branching depth.[45] The work consists of a square of 9 equal squares, 3 by 3. In the center is the parent, and surrounding it, 8 offspring. First generation *Biomorphs* have branches so short they look like dots. Like Sims' *Galápagos*, the user selects one of the offspring to be the new parent and the next generation is generated from that parent, undergoing random "mutations" — alterations of one of the nine parent genes by +1 or -1 — producing eight new offspring. Fascinatingly, in this process, simple tree structures can recursively branch and overlap to form the bodies of insects, and imitate the wings and legs of birds. "When I wrote the program, I never thought that it would evolve anything more than a variety of tree-like shapes. I had hoped for weeping willows, cedars of Lebanon, Lombardy poplars, seaweed, perhaps deer antlers. Nothing in my biologist's intuition, nothing in my 20 years' experience of programming computers, and nothing in my wildest dreams, prepared me for

[fig2-26] Above: A Screenshot of a web tool created according to the Biomoprh concept.
(https://gatc.ca/projects/biomorph.evolve/)
Below: Biormorphs bred by the author.

what actually emerged on the screen. I can't remember exactly when in the sequence it first began to dawn on me that an evolved resemblance to something like an insect was possible. With a wild surmise, I began to breed, generation after generation, from whichever child looked most like an insect. My incredulity grew in parallel with the evolving resemblance." Again, let's note that the results surprised Dawkins himself, the author of the system. Interesting results of unimagined complexity emerged from a relatively simple mechanism. Computers are machines that not only do exactly what you command them to, but also often surprise you with their results. Dawkins says he became so absorbed in *Biomorph* that he forgot to eat or sleep for days. The original system, unfortunately, did not incorporate a mechanism for storing or reproducing the iterations of genetic code he cultivated, so all encounters with beautiful insects and birds there remain one-time events. He no doubt never witnessed many of its greatest achievements.

Maybe this is easier to imagine in two-dimensions. If the *Biomorph* genome consisted of only two numbers, the number of branches and the length of the branches. Imagine how they might populate a two-dimensional plane, *Biomorphs* with similar genes would cluster adjacent to one another. If you were to move along this two-dimensional *Biomorph* plane, vertically or horizontally, you would encounter areas where permutations were concentrated. In one direction, for example, you might find longer branches; in another, shorter branches. In some areas they might more closely resemble weeping willows; in others you might find an area where they more closely resembled scarab beetles. Next, let's suppose that you want to map your evaluation of each area, vertical to this plane. When bee-like *Biomorphs* were a priority, the area where scarab beetles were assembled would be more elevated than an area with weeping willows. Thus, scarab beetle hills, weeping willow lowlands, and honeybee mountains would be born. The task left for you as an explorer would be to climb the mountains in search of still higher places. Once you have mounted the scarab beetle hill, you may need to descend into the bat valley and then look for a trailhead into the Honeybee Mountains.[46] In Dawkins' *Biomorph*, each individual's genome consisted of nine parameters. Therefore, an accurate rendition of a Dawkinian *Biomorph* space would be a nine-dimensional world. I don't know anyone who can actually imagine a nine-dimensional space in their head, so I used two dimensions, but hopefully you, dear reader, can extrapolate and understand that each dimension of *Biomorphs* would be organized according to this same clustering phenomenon we saw in the two-dimensional and three-dimensional versions. Small parameter changes would also make big differences in the shapes produced and their evaluations. Note that the *Biomorph* topography would not always be gentle. There would be cliffs.

Like the librarians in the *Library of Babel*, the person who evolves each *Biomorph* could therefore be likened to an explorer or archeologist in that particular nine-dimensional world. The act of evolving *Bio-*

morphs is equivalent to moving through that nine-dimensional space, in search of genetic structures that express more desirable *Biomorphs*, by whatever criteria. Alternatively, one might say that all manner of viable *Biomorph* potential already existed somewhere in the nine-dimensional space from its inception. It would, in fact, be like exploring a *Genetic Library of Babel*. The numbers of genes in living organisms are much greater than those of a nine-dimensional *Biomorph*, and therefore its *Genetic Library of Babel* would be many orders of magnitude larger. However, once the number of genes is determined, the possible total number of genetic combinations are finite, even if large enough to seem almost infinite. What, then, can we say about looking at the evolution of life and the simulations we saw in this section in terms of the relationship between the *Library of Babel* and creativity? If finite and discrete gene combinations define the search space under review, then mutations, crossovers, and trait inheritances are algorithms for search. Mechanisms of natural selection, whether by viewer preference in *Galápagos* and *Biomorphs*, or evaluation by the speed of movement of virtual creatures in *Evolved Virtual Creatures*, both assess fitness, and suitability for their environment. With the search space, search algorithm, evaluation function, and the time of only billions of years(!), we human beings are among the myriad theoretical species generated on planet Earth.

Cultural genes

The processes of evolution and cultural formation share much in common. Our cultural inheritance, a code which has survived socio-economic changes, adaptations to changing circumstances, and re-combinations, enduring the natural selection of power, popularity, and obsolescence.[47] Just as the *Galápagos* virtual life forms evolved by feeding on the viewer's aesthetics, so has our cultural inheritance been selected, bred, and evolved over generations within us. In his book *The Selfish Gene*, Dawkins popularized (and famously, embarrassingly, anthropomorphized) the idea of a "meme," paralleling the gene, to promote a non-deterministic inclusive fitness in human societies.[48] Self-propagating ideas such as religions, superstitions, myths and legends, national customs, post-national ideas like human rights and democracy, even urban tribes like Mods and Rockers. Some as long as humanity itself, some as short as a Tic-Tok millisecond.

Writing this book in 2020, I was provided ample evidence of biological and sociological evidence of both the genetic propagation of the COVID-19 virus, and memetic propagation of virality, whether in the ability of the medical community to serve its populace, social distancing, or of a heightened sense of global tribalism and awareness of social inequity; each had "outbreaks" and "super-spreader events" in the bodies and minds of the global populace. Styles of painting and genres of music are also memes. The memes that breed in the minds of artists may cross and proliferate with other memes to generate further new memes, but most of them will not go anywhere beyond the artist themselves, and vanish without descendants.

Some artists have created or participated in keeping memes alive through posterity. Picasso is widely known to have collected African masks. He was also interested in Henri Poincaré's multidimensional mathematics and is said to have frequently held study sessions with expert friends.[49] He was also a talented photographer. The convergence of such seemingly disparate memes in Picasso's talent can be seen in *La Femme qui pleure*. This new meme of cubism not only propagated in the minds of many artists of the same era, but shook the concept of art itself, and remains relevant today. In pop music, there is the paradox of the Beatles' *Sergeant Peppers Lonely Hearts Club Band* vs *The Velvet Underground & Nico*. Sgt. Pepper's was lauded from the moment of its release as a "defining moment in 1960s pop culture," and applauded for its artistic merits and for its impact on popular culture, yet over time, its memetic relevance seems surprisingly small. In the same year, *The Velvet Underground & Nico* was released, famously sold only 60,000 copies but has created countless imitators over the succeeding half-century. This is not a statement about the relative qualities of either record, but it does indicate that what is considered popular or important in culture at the time is not necessarily what has the greatest mimetic fitness.

2.7 For AI to generate its own creativity

Colin Martindale was a professor of psychology at the University of Maine, and recognized expert in creativity and artistic processes who saw artists as members of society seeking an evolutionary "arousal potential" for themselves and others through work.[50] Martindale argued that art forms arise from artists' necessity to produce new works to counter the effects of boredom or habituation, eventually leading to a monotonic increase in novelty, unpredictability, and complexity of output, as well as oscillations in content indicative of primary process (autistic, dreamlike) cognition.

British-Canadian psychologist Daniel Ellis Berlyne's work focused on how objects and experiences are influenced by and have an influence on curiosity and arousal.[51] Berlyne used the *Wundt Curve*, a spectrum of Comfort and Discomfort calculated according to Stimulus Intensity, developed by the "father of experimental psychology" Wilhelm Maximilian Wundt to explain human motivations in the realm of aesthetics, seeking to increase various low-level stimuli for increasing senses of reward, in the bell of the curve, and then ambivalence about following it through "novelty," "surprise," "complexity," and "ambiguity" to "confusion" at the edges.[fig2-27] The center of the Wundt Curve, it seems, is boring, but at the extremes "too much is never enough."

This is also convincing in an everyday sense. We are typically caught between our desire for familiar expressions and our desire for new stimulation. The essence of Martindale's theory is that when the force to increase stimulus is slightly stronger, the creative activities of human beings advance. In the minds of artists, the memes of their "influences" and the new memes being generated are always in fierce competition for survival. And the slightly stronger orientation for novelty has generated new styles, methods, and memes that break us out of the confines of past art styles. What if we apply this idea to the realm of AI?

Intuitively, we don't expect innovative creativity from old-school

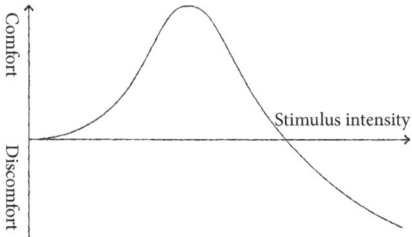

[fig2-27] Wundt curve

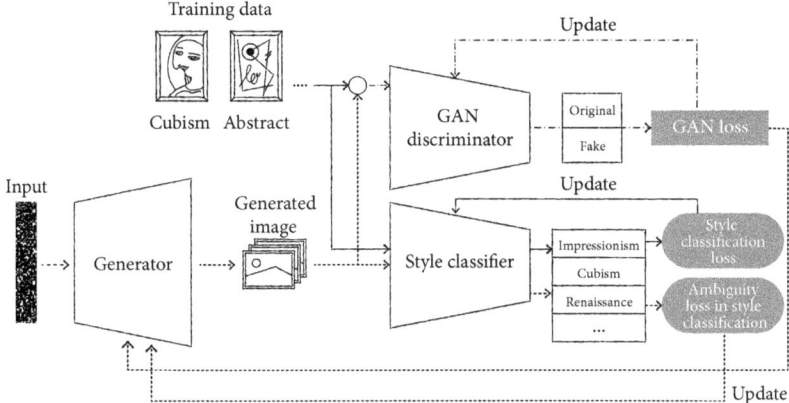

[fig2-28] CAN algorithm diagram

procedural rule-based AI. In supervised ML, the proximity of the output to the model given as training data is the evaluation criterion, and learning proceeds to minimize this difference (error, loss) as far as possible. In an experiment trained on Rembrandt, generating a Picasso is still an error.

Let's assume that you have an ideal GAN that generates only images that look exactly like the paintings contained in the training data, but nothing else. If the outputted images are the same as the training data, the Discriminator would have no way to distinguish them and be fooled. Since the purpose of training the Generator is to deceive the Discriminator, once it becomes possible to generate only images that look exactly like the training data, the GAN learning process is concluded. We can therefore assess that new expressions will not emerge from a general GAN. If something beyond the framework is derived then it should be an error, a bug or an accident. Our key questions are "Can general AI and ML systems similarly surprise even their creators?" "Can AI possess innovative creativity?" and "Can AI lead to previously unimagined ideas and expressions?" Finding new hope in Creative Adversarial Networks (CAN). [fig2-28] [52]

CAN, which was first proposed in 2017 by a research team at Rutgers University led by Ahmed Elgammal, Bingchen Liu, Mohamed Elhoseiny, and Marian Mazzone, is structured much like GANs, with an adversarial setup of generator versus discriminator. However, it has one key addition: another discriminator that classifies the styles of generated images. The generator and discriminators were trained on historical Western paintings in various styles, such as Baroque, Pointillist, Cubist, Rococo, Fauvist, and Abstract Expressionist. The original discriminator still tries to learn how to classify each image as real or fake. But the new discriminator is trained to classify images generated by the generator into one of those styles. We could structure the algorithm to value a Cubist painting more highly (= seen as relatively close to the Cubist style), then more images with Cubist characteristics would be generated. This is called conditioning.

What makes CAN interesting is how it uses the GAN adversarial structure to generate novelty. In the CAN algorithm, images that are "indistinguishable from any style" are more highly valued by the style-identifying classifier. The CAN generator's goal is to confuse the new classifier so that images "indistinguishable as any particular style" are more highly ranked, making the output evenly probable for all styles.[53] While the classifier in the original GAN algorithm was used as is, training the generator to confuse the new Pointillist, Cubist, Rococo, etc., genre classifier while ensuring the "authenticity"[54] of the generated images to the original discriminator produced new paintings.

It is worth noting that by introducing a second classifier while taking advantage of the GAN framework, the aim is to explicitly produce new expressions that deviate from existing ones. Instead of waiting for something to emerge by chance, the model was intentionally modified to produce it. The images generated were abstract, and it is interesting that the result of learning from and learning to avoid expressions from Western art history generated abstract expressionism.[fig2-29]

In 2016 university art students were surveyed by the Rutgers group, to assess whether a human or a computer had created the images of GAN, CAN, historical Abstract Expressionist works, and non-figurative work on view at Art Basel. The Abstract Expressionist works were rated the highest, with 85 percent of respondents correctly identifying them as the work of a human artist. Yet the students believed that 53 percent of the CAN images were made by humans, as compared to only 35 percent of the GAN images, and 41 percent of the Art Basel works. More tellingly, the art students "rated the images generated by the computer higher than those created by real artists, whether in the Abstract Expressionism set or in the Art Basel set."

Applying Martindale's theories of "arousal potential" to counter the effects of boredom or habituation, and increase novelty, unpredictability, and complexity of output, then we might say that the CAN learned its way out of the rut of cultural inheritance, and evolved to generate images of greater arousal potential, considered new, and relatively

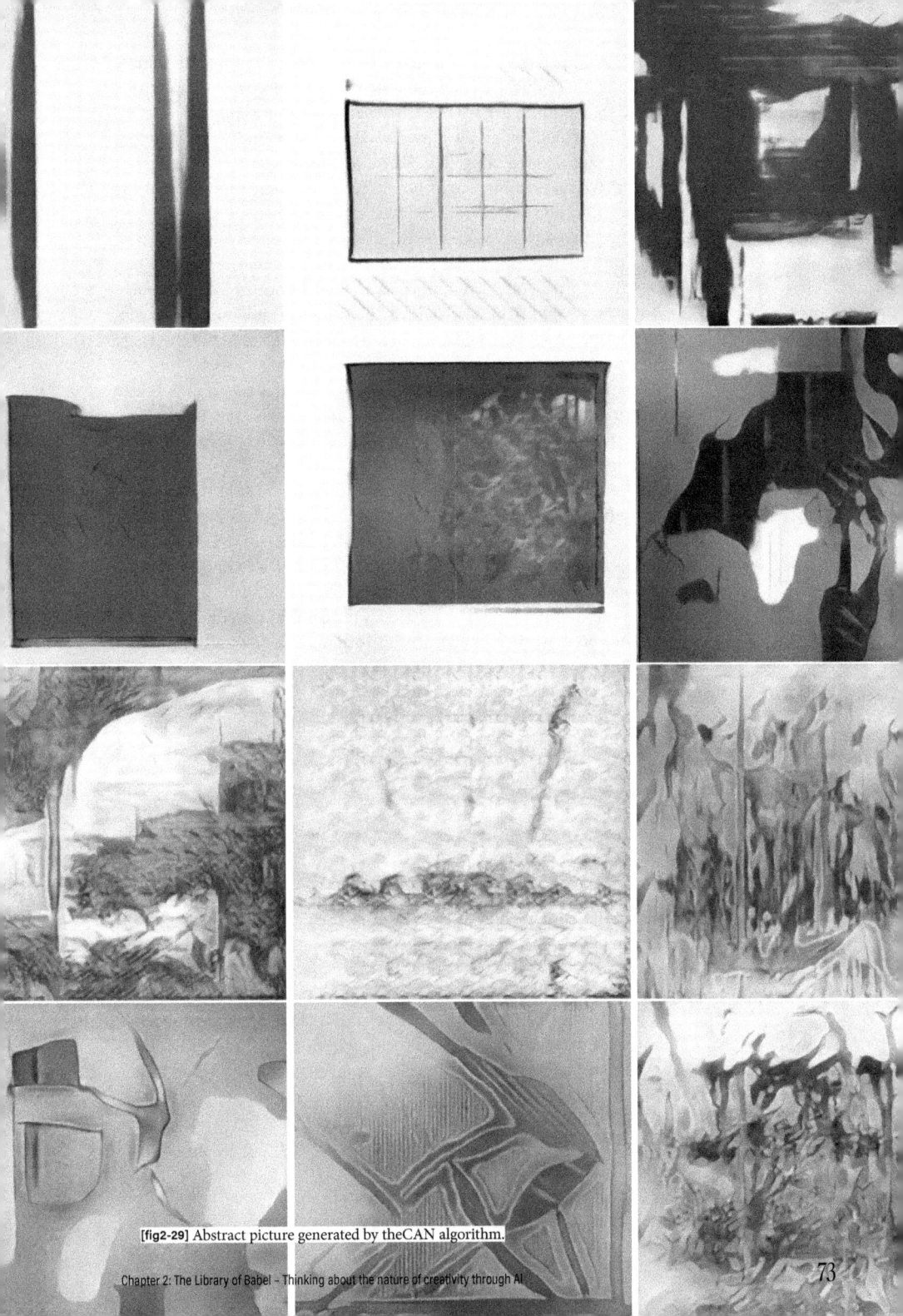

[fig2-29] Abstract picture generated by theCAN algorithm.

valuable by a majority of those sampled. Particular attention should be paid to the "ambiguity" among multiple stimulating elements. Everyone remembers their first experience with pictures, music, and other artistic expressions which defied all previous experiences, and were therefore confusing and exhilarating. It's often hard to evaluate the "new," but the novelty of expression might be indirectly evaluated in terms of the ambiguity and sense of intrigue we face at that moment.

This also applies to the world of music. Artists who create new styles always fall between the cracks of existing classifications. When Aphex Twin and Autechre emerged at the beginning of the 1990s, record stores couldn't imagine which shelf to put them on.[55] I first discovered Autechre in the punk rock section! Curious to apply the CAN framework to music, I began a series of experiments to apply the CAN algorithm to rhythm generation, hoping to create a new dance music sub-genre. Electronic dance music is a field where new sub-genres such as jungle, drum'n'bass, 2-step (two-step), dubstep, trap, and juke, house, and techno have been generated almost every year since the 1990s.[56] Each sub-genre is characterized by a unique rhythm pattern and rhythmic groove. So can AI generate new rhythm patterns and, consequently, new dance music sub-genres? I collected MIDI data from rhythm patterns in multiple genres and used a relatively simple GAN architecture to generate new rhythms. For nine types of drums, including kicks, snares, and hi-hats, I developed a model that generates presence or absence on a two-bar 9x32 grid with 16th notes as the minimum unit. Preliminary experiments show that adding genre-specific input conditions generates rhythm patterns unique to each genre. Adding a second classifier to identify genre, like with CAN, and built a mechanism to confuse this classifier generated unique dance music rhythm patterns![57] It was like listening to tracks from different state-of-the-art electronic dance music labels.[58]

Meme seeds

Section 2.2 introduced the concept of Transformational Creativity, creativity which expands the realm of the concept and exploration space itself. CAN is a study aimed at realizing this goal, by pursuing Transformational Creativity which breaks from past styles to generate unprecedented work.

While the generated images look like abstract paintings, the creativity of the CAN algorithm remains within the parameters initially set by the researchers. Doing the same experiment with paintings before the 1910s would only produce abstract expressions, but neither Picasso nor Braque. No Duchamp *Fountain* would result. In my experiment, it wasn't possible for the system to generate finer rhythms than the grid limit of 16th note units, in triplets, or shuffled rhythms such as 2-step.

I think that this work is very important in the sense that AI itself has suggested the possibility of producing new memetic substances.

In the future, there will no doubt be gardeners who carefully cultivate memes produced by AI to generate large new flowers worthy of Boden's historical creativity. The fruits thus obtained will be added to generate new collections within the *Library of Babel*. And as the seeds left by the flowers are passed on to the next generation, the memes that originated in AI may occupy a part of our cultural meme ecosystem.

In this chapter, we worked on describing creativity from a non-human perspective, from the viewpoint of computers, AI, and evolution. Through the *Library of Babel* metaphor we saw creative practices modeled as exploration in the space of possibilities and activities that seek to expand that space itself. We questioned whether computers can be creative, based on premises laid down by Lovelace and Turing. We introduced evolutionary simulations and algorithms that extend GAN as proof that computers can surprise people. Speaking of creativity in the words of AI not only suggests that creativity can be fully expanded using AI, but also gives us a new perspective on creativity. Tools and mirrors: this is the duality of AI. I hope that the reader understood my intention, written in chapter 1, "It is important to recognize the nature of AI as a tool, and then dare to focus on elements that are not just tools of AI and think about how to make maximum use of them."

In the next chapter, we will go back in time and take a bird's-eye view of the history of "imitation" machines. How did human beings treat machines as tools and mirrors to reflect themselves in the past? Let's explore the future of human relationships with AI, by learning to observe different aspects of historical imitation machines.

Endnotes

1. J. L. Borges, *Fictions* (Grove Press for English translation, 1962)
   The idea for the comparison with the *Library of Babel* was suggested in my interview with Shohei Matsukawa, associate professor at Keio University SFC. I also referred to the following book in which the author had a fictional interview with Borges.
   Kevin Kelly, *Out of Control: The New Biology of Machines, Social Systems, and the Economic World* (Basic Books, 1992)
2. The *Neverending Story* by Michael Ende is similar. The episode features a monkey, who entertains people, young and old, male and female, by letting them play a game of dice with letters on them, to produce sentences, stories, or poems by pure chance. The author is using the Infinite monkey theorem -- the idea that an infinite number of monkeys randomly hitting keys on a typewriter keyboard for an infinite amount of time will eventually produce the complete works of Shakespeare.
3. Ben Parr, Google: There Are 129,864,880 Books in the Entire World (Mashable, 08.2010)
   https://mashable.com/archive/number-of-books-in-the-world
4. This is an example of a binary search.
5. When you take the rhythm for four—four time, "1 and 2 and 3 and 4 and...", "and" is the backbeat.
6. Colin Martindale, *Clockwork Muse* (Basic Books, 1990)
7. Generally, the evaluation function is part of the search algorithm. I'm separating the two here, for clearer exposition.
8. Richard Dawkins, *The Blind Watchmaker: Why the Evidence of Evolution Reveals a Universe without Design* (Norton & Company, 1986)
9. Japan Creative Society, *The definition of creation*
   http://www.japancreativity.jp/definition.html
   Makoto Takahashi, *The Bible of Creativity -- "Creative Methods" to develop Japanese creativity covering main 88 techniques!* (Nikkagiren, 2002)
10. Margaret A. Boden, *Computer Models of Creativity*, AI Magazine, Vol.30 No.3 (7.2009)
    Margaret A. Boden, *The Creative Mind: Myths and Mechanisms: Second Edition* (Routledge, 2003)
11. *The Unreasonable Effectiveness of Recurrent Neural Networks*, Andrej Karpathy Blog (5.2015)
    https://karpathy.github.io/2015/05/21/rnn-effectiveness/
12. Alec Radford, Jeffrey Wu, Dario Amodei, Daniela Amodei, Jack Clark, Miles Brundage, Ilya Sutskever, *Better Language Models and Their Implications* (OpenAI, 2.2019)
    https://openai.com/research/better-language-models
13. GPT-3, *A robot wrote this entire article. Are you scared yet, human?* (8/2020)
    https://www.theguardian.com/commentisfree/2020/sep/08/robot-wrote-this-article-gpt-3
14. Janelle Shane, *You Look Like a Thing and I Love You: How Artificial Intelligence Works and Why It's Making the World a Weirder Place* (Little, Brown and Company, 2019) The title of the book itself is also generated by charRNN.
15. Robin Sloan, *Writing with the Machine* (5.2016)
    https://www.robinsloan.com/notes/writing-with-the-machine/
16. Matthew Braga, *The Verbasizer Was David Bowie's 1995 Lyric-Writing Mac App* (VICE, 1.2016)
    https://www.vice.com/en/article/xygxpn/theverbasizer-was-david-bowies-1995-lyricwriting-mac-app
17. BBC News, *How David Bowie used 'cut ups' to create lyrics* (1.2016)
    https://www.youtube.com/watch?v=6nlW4EbxTD8
18. Jean-Pierre Briot, Gaëtan Hadjeres, François-David Pachet, *Deep Learning*

Techniques for Music Generation (Springer, 2019)
19 Douglas Eck, Jürgen Schmidhuber, *A First Look at Music Composition Using LSTM Recurrent Neural Networks* (IDSIA, 7.2002)
20 Ian Simon, Sageev Oore, *Performance RNN: Generating Music with Expressive Timing and Dynamics* (Magenta Blog, 01.2017)
https://magenta.tensorflow.org/performance-rnn
Sageev Oore, Ian Simon, Sander Dieleman, Douglas Eck, Karen Simonyan, *This Time with Feeling: Learning Expressive Musical Performance* / arXiv:1808.03715v1 [cs.SD] (8.2018)
21 Abbreviation for Musical Instrument Digital Interface, a 1981 communications protocol for connecting electronic musical devices and computers developed by Ikutaro Kakehashi of Roland Corporation (and inventor of the TR-808 Rhythm Composer) and Dave Smith of Sequential Circuits. Since it's invention MIDI has become a common standard for transferring and sharing performance data between electronic musical devices.
22 http://www.piano-e-competition.com/
23 The MAESTRO Dataset
https://magenta.tensorflow.org/datasets/maestro
24 Soroush Mehri, Kundan Kumar, Ishaan Gulrajani, Rithesh Kumar, Shubham Jain, Jose Sotelo, Aaron Courville, Yoshua Bengio, *SampleRNN: An Unconditional End-to-End Neural Audio Generation Model* / arXiv:1612.07837v2 [cs.SD] (2017)
25 The μ-law sound compression algorithm used in telephone communication.
26 The generated "album" is available via Bandcamp.
https://dadabots.bandcamp.com/
27 Aaron van den Oord, Sander Dieleman, Heiga Zen, Karen Simonyan, Oriol Vinyals, Alex Graves, Nal Kalchbrenner, Andrew Senior, Koray Kavukcuoglu, *WaveNet: A Generative Model for Raw Audio* / arXiv:1609.03499v2 [cs.SD] (2016)
28 https://deepmind.com/blog/article/wavenet-launches-google-assistant
When the paper was first published, it took nearly a minute to synthesize a second of speech, but now processes more than 1000x faster.
29 For the anecdotes of Babbage and Ada, I referred to the following:
Bruce Collier, *Charles Babbage: And the Engines of Perfection* (Oxford University Press, 1999)
Masaaki Shindo, *Babbage's Computer* (Chikuma Shobo, 1996)
Toru Nishigaki, *Digital Narcissus-The Desire of Information Science Pioneers* (Iwanami Shoten, 2008)
30 Christopher D. Green, *Charles Babbage, the Analytical Engine, and the Possibility of a 19th-Century Cognitive Science* (York University, 2001)
31 L.F. Menabrea, Luigi Federico, Ada Lovelace, *Sketch of the Analytical Engine Invented by Charles Babbage* (1842)(Independently published, 3.2020)
32 Excerpted: J. Fuegi, J. Francis, *Lovelace & Babbage and the Creation of the 1843 'Notes',* IEEE Annals of the History of Computing Vol.25 (2003)
33 Doron Swade, *Charles Babbage and His Calculating Engines* (Science Museum, 1998)
34 Whereas Neumann anthropomorphised, using the word 'memory', Babbage used agrarian words such as 'storehouse' and 'millstone'. What Babbage had in mind was something like the jacquard loom he had seen in Paris, not a machine with human-like intelligence.
35 Pamela McCorduck, *Machines Who Think: A Personal Inquiry Into the History and Prospects of Artificial Intelligence* (W. H. Freeman & Co., 1979)
36 Steven Johnson, *Emergence: The Connected Lives of Ants, Brains, Cities and Software* (Scribner, 2001)
37 A method of inferring overall tendencies from the ratio to the population parameter by investigating only a partial survey of all subjects.
38 Karl Sims, *Galápagos* (1997)
https://www.ntticc.or.jp/ja/archive/works/galapagos/
39 NTT InterCommunication No.21 1997 Summer (NTT Publishing, 1997)

40 Peter J. Bentley, *Evolutionary Design by Computers* (Morgan Kaufmann, 1999) Hitoshi Iba, *Basics of Genetic Algorithms-Solving the Mystery of GA* (Ohmsha, 1994)
41 Karl Sims, *Evolving Virtual Creatures* / SIGGRAPH '94: Proceedings of the 21st annual conference on Computer graphics and interactive techniques (7.1994)
42 Consider John Searle's Chinese Room thought experiment. A person outside of a room is having a conversation in Chinese text with an unknown person through a door. Every time the person outside asks a question in Chinese, an appropriate answer is returned, in Chinese, so the person outside comes to the conclusion that the person inside understands Chinese. In fact, the person inside the room has no knowledge of Chinese, can not read Chinese characters, but simply writes and returns messages according to a rule book based on Chinese inputs in the questions. Imagine replacing the person in the room with an AI model performing the Turing test.
43 Selmer Bringsjord, Paul Bello, David Ferrucci, *Creativity, the Turing Test, and the (Better) Lovelace Test* / Minds and Machines 11 (2.2001)
44 Richard Dawkins, *The Blind Watchmaker-Is Natural Selection a coincidence?* (Norton & Company, Inc. 1896)
45 Regarding biomorphs, I also refer to Kevin Kelly's commentary in *Out of Control: the New Instead: Biology of Machines, Social Systems, and the Economic World* (Basic Books, 1992)
46 The state after you can no longer climb higher is called "falling into a local solution". For deep learning models, the training proceeds in the direction of minimizing error. In this analogy, it is like searching a valley for its lowest possible point (gradient descent method).
47 Alex Mesudi, *Cultural Evolution-How Darwinian Theory Can Explain Human Culture and Synthesize the Social Sciences* (University of Chicago, 2011)
48 Richard Dawkins, *The Selfish Gene* (Oxford University Press, 1976)
49 Arthur I. Miller, *Einstein, Picasso: space, time, and the beauty that causes havoc* (Basic Books, 2001)
50 Colin Martindale, *The Clockwork Muse: The Predictability of Artistic Change* (BasicBooks, 1990)
51 D. E. Berlyne, *Aesthetics and Psychobiology* (Appleton-Century-Crofts, 1971)
52 Ahmed Elgammal, Bingchen Liu, Mohamed Elhoseiny, Marian Mazzone, *CAN: Creative Adversarial Networks, Generating "Art" by Learning About Styles and Deviating from Style Norms* / arXiv:1706.07068v1 [cs.AI] (2017)
53 In technical terms, the goal is to increase the cross entropy of the style classifier.
54 Please note that I'm only referring to Western painting data sets.
55 Perhaps this is such a book.
56 *Ishkur's Guide to Electronic Music* (https://music.ishkur.com/)
You can browse the phylogenetic tree of nearly 100 genres while listening to actual music on this site.
57 You can listen to a generated rhythm example on the web page.
RhythmCAN - Generating novel rhythm patterns using GAN with Genre Ambiguity Loss (https://cclab.sfc.keio.ac.jp/projects/rhythmcan/)
58 Hessle Audio and Whities are two of my favorite labels.

Chapter —— 3

A history of AI, simulacra, and simulation

3.1 Edison's Turing Test

The speaking machine

"Only God can produce words, and trying to compete with God by believing that he has such power is a terrible blasphemy," said a 19C nobleman to the young engineer trying to make a "speaking machine." "Yes" he continued — and his voice choked up the more he tried to make it strong — "you have set down all that the others know and the greater part of what they dream about; but I am greater. I can, to borrow from Poe, create worlds in movement, and blazing, roaring spheres with the sound from matter without a soul; and I have surpassed Lucifer in that I can force inorganic things to blaspheme. Night and day, according to my will, skins which were alive, and metals which perhaps are not yet so, utter lifeless words; and if it is true that the voice creates universes in space, those that I have caused it to create are worlds that have died before they came to life. In my house lies a behemoth that bellows at a wave of my hand; *I have invented a talking machine*." Marcel Schwob, *The Talking Machine: a Tale à la Poe via Thomas A. Edison*, 23 août 1867

In fact, a number of contemporaneous inventors were competing to produce devices and different means of recording and reproducing sound in different ways.[1]

Émile-Hortensius-Charles Cros, the South American noble, poet, and inventor, may have been the first person to conceive of a method for reproducing recorded sound, in his hauntingly named the paleophone, or voix du passé ("voice of the past"). Cros got the idea while working on technology to colorize black-and-white photographs. Yet, it was Thomas Edison who, on November 21, 1877, first commercialized the invention that could both record and reproduce sound: the phonograph. Edison's invention came from attempts to play back recorded telegraph messages and to automate speech sounds for transmission by telephone. Telegraphic signals could be relayed at thirty-five to forty words a minute; but with a phonograph several hundred words a minute were possible. And this proved a decisive advantage.

Today, we assume that gramophones, records, and CDs exist to play recorded music. In 1878, Edison listed the following uses for his invention:

1. Letter writing, and all kinds of dictation without the aid of a stenographer.
2. Photographic books, which will speak to blind people without effort on their part.
3. The teaching of elocution.
4. Music – the phonograph will undoubtedly be liberally devoted to music.
5. The family record; preserving the sayings, the voices, and the last words of the dying members of the family, as of great men.
6. Music boxes, toys, etc. – A doll which may speak, sing, cry or laugh may be promised to our children for the Christmas holidays ensuing.
7. Clocks, that should announce in speech the hour of the day, call you to lunch, send your lover home at ten, etc.
8. The preservation of language by reproduction of our Washingtons, our Lincolns, our Gladstones.
9. Educational purposes; such as preserving the instructions of a teacher so that the pupil can refer to them at any moment; or learn spelling lessons.
10. The perfection or advancement of the telephone's art by the phonograph, making that instrument an auxiliary in the transmission of permanent records.

Edison clearly conceived of the device to add value to existing technologies like print, clocks, the electrical telegraph, and photography. Telephony had just been invented. Photography was still only a generation old. The phonograph, in addition to providing a pragmatic record for communications on the one-to-one telephone, was imagined as a tool in the service of social mobility, facilitating the reading of books, aiding elocution and education, bringing classical music to the masses, communicating the wisdom of great men, and of deceased family members. Music, and entertainment, are only mentioned twice. The companies created to exploit the phonograph, such as Victor Talking Machines and Consolidated Talking Machines emphasized that it was imagined to exist for a linguistic function. Words, grammar, meaning: not just vibrations in air.

In early demonstrations Edison famously used a recording of *Mary Had a Little Lamb*, played at various speeds, generating high and low voices to simulate different genders. (The gramophone at that time had to be rotated by hand using the handle, so cranking slower or faster facilitated this *Imitation Game*.) A pre-recorded cornet performance was also part of the demonstration, and again, cranked faster and slower demonstrated music in registers above and below what that instrument could actually produce.

[fig3-1] Magazine advertisement by Victor Talking Machine (1908)

[fig3-2] *His Master's Voice*

Even though virtually all of the data about those involved in the development of these machines, and their use, demonstrates a rational understanding that these machines were using physics to reproduce sound, culturally, the phenomenon illustrated in the opening quote was common at that time. Somehow, there was a parallel general anxiety about machines taking over roles formerly performed by the human voice. Much like today's misconceptions about AI. Even though it only recorded sound waves in the air, culturally it was regarded as a mechanical imitation of the ability to speak words (grammar, syntax, etc.) and by inference, that human ability. As though a deceased person's voice would be therein "reanimated."

As quality improved, multiple gramophone manufacturers created a market, and the promotions for these Talking Machine companies came to emphasize audio fidelity. In a 1908 advertisement for Victor Talking Machines, opera megastar Enrico Caruso and the company's gramophone are lined up, with the slogan "Which is which?" insinuating that having the record is like having Caruso himself perform in your home — because the reproduction would be indistinguishable from his live performance.[fig3-1] This was familiar to consumers because Edison Phonograph was known for conducting tone tests in which live singers alternated with recordings before a blindfolded audience.[2] One might consider this to be Edison's own Turing test for high-fidelity audio.

His Master's Voice (1898) is one of the most famous logos of all time, an image that symbolizes this overlap between recording as mimicry and authenticity.[fig3-2] The story in publicity was that a terrier-mix named Nipper had originally been the beloved pet of painter Francis Barraud's brother, Mark. After Mark passed away, Francis inherited Nipper, along with a cylinder phonograph and recordings of Mark's voice. One day, at his studio at 92 Bold Street, Liverpool, Francis was listening to his brother using the device, and noticed a peculiar interest that the dog took in hearing the recorded voice of his late master emanating from the horn. The logo is the result of Francis' depiction of this

[fig3-3] Advertisement against "canned music" posted by a group of musicians(1930)

moment.[3] Dogs have famously excellent hearing, so Nipper, ear cocked, epitomized this blurring of recording and presence of the recorded individual. It's worth noting that this was a mere 40 years from the time when a Talking Machine could be credibly portrayed as "surpassing Lucifer... I can force inorganic things to blaspheme" crossing into the uncanny valley, until it transformed into a globally beloved icon of a dog's faithful love. How long, I wonder, until AI is able to serve as a medium for the deceased?

As recording technology improved, and recorded music distribution became established, gramophones eventually became specialized machines for music reproduction. Music recorded on vinyl was initially called "canned" music,[4] a blasphemy of "real" music.[fig3-3] Today when we "listen to music" we generally mean recorded music. Otherwise, we use the word "live." Recorded music was first elevated to an art form by autodidact, musician, and inventor Les Paul. While still in his early teens, he experimented with electrifying his acoustic guitar by wiring a phonograph needle to his guitar, and connected it to a radio speaker. He later went on to innovate the solid-body electric guitar. His experiments with overdubbing, tape delay, phasing, and multitrack recording changed recorded music from a documentary into a plastic art form.

As magnetic tapes came to be used for recording, new methods for cutting and pasting sounds appeared.[5] Pianist Glenn Gould who retired from live performance at age 32 to focus on recording was known for his innovations, playing multiple takes of a given composition, then cutting and pasting the best together to achieve truly ideal recorded versions. Of course, no discussion of the plasticity of recording would be complete without mentioning the Beach Boys' *Pet Sounds*, and the Beatles' *Sergeant Pepper's Lonely Hearts Club Band*[6], the cultural call-and-response which fully established the recording studio as an instrument in its own right, and introduced avant-garde techniques of multi-tracking, cut-and-paste, reversed recording, and sound collage art techniques within some of the most commercially successful and creatively influential projects of their time.

Today, as sound recording has largely left magnetic tape and become entirely digital, techniques like virtual instruments and pitch-corrected vocals using Auto-Tune[7] have become commonplace. And this, in fact, has led to live concert performances increasingly supported by what were formerly studio technologies. Recording has ceased to be the faithful capture of "his master's voice," and instead become a kind of idealized fiction built around other promotional elements of an actual singer or performer. Take for example "virtual" bands such as Gorillaz presenting their fictional universe on the same terms as actual performers. I have to imagine that some smart artist will soon manage to integrate AI "mimicry" into pop music vocabulary. It of course remains to be seen if events like Tupac's hologram at Coachella with Snoop Dogg become a more common occurrence, but I don't believe that was the last we'll see of that sort of thing. The technology exists. Deepfake videos using face synthesis technology offer new creative opportunities and call for new legal remedies. The recognition that recorded sound and imagery are no longer rooted in reality, leads toward a more appropriate sense of distance from such imitations generated by AI.

3.2 (AI Hibari Misora) Doppelgangers and impersonators

"In a word, it's blasphemy."

It would be hard to overstate the importance of NHK *Kouhaku Uta Gassen* (= the Singing Battle of Red vs White) to a non-Japanese. Google tells me that *Dick Clark's Rockin' Eve* is a TV show Americans traditionally watched to ring in the New Year. And before that, *Guy Lombardo from the Waldorf Astoria*. In the UK, the BBC has fireworks. It's hard to imagine that they compare.

Firstly, Japan is the nation that invented karaoke. We really truly do love singing socially. Secondly, red and white are the colors of the Japanese flag, representing the two dominant Imperial warrior clans from almost a millennia ago. And if that wasn't enough to draw the battle lines, the Red team are all women, and the White team are all men. NHK is our public broadcaster, like the BBC, and this has been their biggest show, every year, since 1953. Performers only appear by invitation. Preceding MTV by more than a generation, a great performance on *Kohaku* is an immaculately documented historical highlight of any singer's career. Everybody watches or listens (it is simulcast on the radio) for four hours as 25 singers from each team, virtually all singers of note for that year, perform set pieces featuring over-the-top costumes, hairstyles, makeup, choreography, and lighting, as Japan counts down to the end of the year. At the end, a panel of judges and audience members declare a "winner."

Hibari Misora will similarly be hard to describe to a non-Japanese. Imagine a hybrid of Shirley Temple and Edith Piaf. She defined her era from the time she was a child, and growing up to become the cool girl every woman or man could relate to, and would want to party with. When she sang, the clouds parted. She understood you. Everything was going to work out, despite the odds. She died at age 52. Her records still sell well 40 years later. As of today, she's sold in excess of 100 million.

From 1949 until 1971, she appeared in 160 movies, and most Japanese born before the 1970s feel nothing but nostalgia seeing any one of them again. She was a fixture on *Kouhaku* between 1957 and 1973 when her brother was prosecuted for organized crime-related activity, and she was excluded. She then refused to appear on NHK again, in any capacity, for years.

30 years after her death, for the 2019 NHK *Kouhaku Uta Gassen*, Hibari Misora appeared as a hologram, singing *Arekara* (Thereafter), a new song, her vocals generated by Yamaha's *Vocaloid: AI*. The AI was the result of painstaking craft, a production followed by NHK crews, and made into tv specials that year. The lyrics were written by Yasushi Akimoto, the lyricist responsible for her swansong mega-hit *Kawa no nagare no yō ni (*Like the river flows*)*, and the song itself was composed by young singer-songwriter Kafu Sato. I'm sure the vetting process was intense. Every imaginable respect was paid to her legacy. Her voice was generated by Yamaha engineers using DL, based on the vocal tracks from many of some 1,200 songs she recorded in her lifetime, studying each element of her particular delivery and intonation. One line in the song, "It's been a long time. How are you?" was taken directly from a message left on her son's answering machine. Fans were moved by the semblance, its verisimilitude triggered associations with who she was to them. But some SNS were more caustic, including comments like "blasphemy," etc by a beloved cultural figure, as referenced above.[8] As entertainment, maybe part of the offense taken was that it was a "straight" impersonation, no wink-wink, nudge-nudge which, I suppose, is often added to give people an opportunity to create emotional distance and not take things personally. Everyone involved with the project was evidently too focused on accurately reproducing Hibari. Obviously, using information about the deceased without permission is culturally unacceptable, but her family was involved. With public figures there is often a sense of ownership among fans, and posthumous releases of a musician's unfinished outtakes are always problematic. But this was different.

Hitoshi Matsubara, former chairman of the Japanese Society for Artificial Intelligence, raises a thought-provoking question: "Why criticize a machine for impersonation? Would we have criticized a human for doing the same thing?" I believe this is an essential problem concerning universal machines, the concept of impersonation, and the realm in which artificial intelligence exists. If the term AI was replaced with "CG ventriloquism," insinuating an intricate mechanism of strings and levers manipulating a physical form alongside teams of computer hologram experts, would the offense be as "blasphemous?" On a spectrum of simulacra, why don't people see AI as a form of impersonation? Why do we anthropomorphize human traits or intentions on non-humans at all? In fact, AI is modeled on human intelligence. But at the same time, it is also useful to teach us about other forms of intelligence. Where does impersonation meet blasphemy? Why do we play with dolls or channel our emotions through actors, people pretending to be someone they are not, on stage and screen? Every actor adds and subtracts elements, deformations, which make their portrayals more vivid in our perception than the person himself. Take Key and Peele's *Obama's anger translator* skit, for example, saying things President Obama never said and would never say, which still resonate with the viewer because the audience can easily suspend disbelief and imagine that he should. Sasha Baron Cohen can play Borat as high camp, or he can play Abbie Hoffman straight. Both are performed to specific places within the audience's receptivity to that particular character, within that artwork, on a spectrum between impersonation and blasphemy. Universal machines, impersonation, AI, and every performer attempting verisimilitude are all mapping the uncanny valley, a relation of resemblance to someone, but more importantly, our emotional responses to that person.

AI is merely the latest in a series of technologies of imitation and automation of what had previously been accomplished manually. Recall that evolution was also caused by the inheritance of the parent's individual traits through the gene and the addition of minor copy errors (mutations).

3.3 A failure to replicate changed global pop

Vocaloid and electronic musical instruments

An interesting contrast to the blasphemy questions about AI Hibari Misora is the cult of the VOCALOID Hatsune Miku. Both are based on the same Yamaha voice synthesis technology. The Macintosh public beta for OSX was released in 2000, but it took until Mac OS X 10.2 Jaguar, in 2002, before developers were able to rewrite their code, and home studio DAW (Digital Audio Workstation) production was revolutionized: Cubase, Digital Performer, and Pro Tools all released new high-resolution versions, and every audio plug in also updated within a year or so, creating a completely new landscape of creative possibilities. VOCALOID's initial 2003 release didn't have much impact within the DAW community. Today it's commonplace and accepted, but in 2003, the fact that the voice sound source was synthetic wasn't even a sales point. Note the package's "cyber" design.[fig3-4] Yamaha positioned it as a generic option, no doubt intending to offer a maximum latitude for users. Even then, sales were still disappointing.[9]

In 2007, Crypton Future Media released Hatsune Miku, a software voicebank initially inspired and based on the popular anime theme song *chanteuse* Saki Fujita. This innovation, officially known as CV01 in the VOCALOID series, introduced an official *moe*(related to neoteny, evoking an idealization of cuteness, innocence, or vulnerability) anthropomorphism—a young woman with long, turquoise twintails to accompany it. At that time VOCALOID technology was rudimentary, making the anime-inspired conceit work well: Unshackled from any pretense

 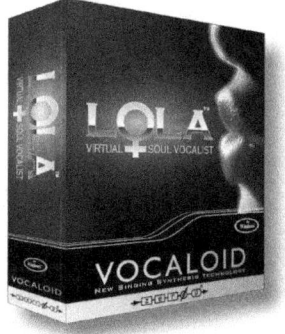

[fig3-4]
Early *Vocaloid* package

of impersonating any specific individual, it felt more natural (?) to adjust the vocal parameters. Users felt free to train "her" like one might customize any online avatar. Just as badly as AI Hibari Misora failed to match the unmatchable Hibari Misora, so Hatsune Miku succeeded in foregrounding her artificiality and gaining a vast and devoted fan base. To date she has featured in more than 100,000 songs released worldwide and has even starred in an opera called *The End*, with music by Keiichiro Shibuya, and costumes by Louis Vuitton, which was performed at the Palais Garnier - Opéra national de Paris opera house.

Ikutaro Kakehashi and electronic music

Ikutaro Kakehashi did as much as anyone to shape electronic music in the 20C, and his legacy is one of leaning hard into artificiality. Most of his inventions were originally spurned before going on to create multiple new genres and generally revolutionize contemporary music. Born in 1930 in Osaka, Japan, both of his parents died of tuberculosis when he was two years old, and he was raised by his grandparents. During the war, he worked on miniature wartime submarines in the Osaka shipyards. After the war, his family moved back to rural Kyushu where, at age 16, he taught himself to repair wristwatches, then radios, and taught himself electronics. At the age of 20, he returned to Osaka to enter university, only to catch tuberculosis and be sent to a sanatorium, where he spent the next four years supporting himself by continuing to repair watches and electronics as his health failed. At age 24, he volunteered to test a new antibiotic, streptomycin. His life was saved, he left the sanatorium, got married, and established the Kakehashi Radio shop in Osaka. Four years later, he decided to devote himself to creating affordable electronic musical instruments.

Kakehashi founded Ace Tone in 1960 to produce electronic organs and early drum machines, including the popular 1964 *R1 Rhythm*

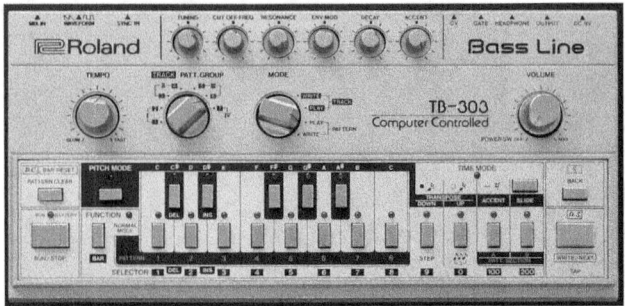

[fig3-5] Roland TB-303

Ace push-button electronic percussion box. He went on to found Roland Corporation in 1972 and was involved in the development of various influential electronic instruments, including the 1974 Roland *RE-201 Space Echo* delay and reverb, and the first guitar synthesizer. His 1978 *Roland CR-78* debuted in the hit *In the Air Tonight*, the first solo single by English drummer and singer-songwriter Phil Collins, and went on to be used in many others. His 1980 Roland *TR-808 Rhythm Composer* was one of the first drum machines which enabled users to program rhythms instead of using preset patterns. Unlike its competitors, the *TR-808* generated sounds using analog synthesis, rather than recorded samples. Featured in hits from *Sexual Healing* by Marvin Gaye, *Planet Rock* by Afrika Bambaataa and the Soulsonic Force, to the present day, famously Ye's *808s & Heartbreak*, it has been used on more hit records than any other drum machine. The "squelching" or "chirping" sound of his 1981 Roland *TB-303 Bass Line* synthesizer,[10] first popularized in 1987 with the song *Acid Tracks* arguably created the "acid house" genre and became a foundation of genres including Chicago house, techno, trance, jungle, and big beat.[fig3-5] In 1991, Kakehashi was awarded an honorary doctorate in music by the Berklee College of Music for his achievements in the development and popularization of electronic musical instruments, and in 2013, shared a Technical Grammy Award with Dave Smith of Sequential as a co-creator of Musical Instrument Digital Interface (MIDI).

Both the *TR-808* and *TB-303* were discontinued after short initial production runs. The critics complained that they weren't lifelike enough. But both, in the hands of musicians who knew where to place them on that mimicry spectrum, saw them make musical history and become valuable collectors' items. It was these machines' limitations that led users to create highly addictive simple looping bass lines. It was precisely the unique and futuristic lack of drum-ness in the *TR-808* that led to its broad adoption throughout hip-hop.[11] In fact, the initial *TR-808*'s distinctive thick bass is said to be due to the use of cheap transistors because, in addition to saving money, the lack of fidelity was found to make interesting noise, like distortion can in amplified guitars.[12] According to Rolling Stone magazine, "the *TR-808* became to hip-hip what the Fender Stratocaster was to rock."[13] The kick drum and unique snare inhabiting the bass-ment of the *TR-808* contributed to the birth of dance music genres such as electro and drum'n'bass. From the aforementioned Marvin Gaye to Kanye West, Diplo, Daft Punk, Pico Taro… on and on, spaceship *TR-808* has traversed all boundaries, known and unknown universes of pop music. To quote Rolling Stone magazine again, "It's almost impossible to imagine what the modern music scene would have been like without the *TR-808*'s signature sound."

Kakehashi's inventions were designed to replace drums, organs, and keyboards, but in fact served to function as markers, placeholders' opening opportunities for similar expressions. His facsimile generated parallel worlds and alternate universes which, in turn, shed light on the distinctive value of the original human ingenuity of percussive ingenuity. From a market perspective, the TB-303 and TR-808—initially priced at $395 and $1195 and originally considered commercial disappointments—have become highly sought-after collector›s items, commanding five to ten times those prices on resale markets today.

3.4 Photography and painting — Imitation ≥ flattery

Pictorial trajectories[14]

Probably the easiest, most recognizable disruptive creative revolution was the camera replacing painters. The daguerreotype, developed by Louis Daguerre of France, was the world's first practical photographic technology.[fig3-6] From the first known human graphic depictions, circa roughly 700,000 BCE, until 1839, every picture any human had seen had been drawn by hand. Precursors include the camera obscura, a mechanism in which light from an external scene passes through a hole in a darkened room (camera=room obscura=shadowy) and strikes a surface inside, where the information in the reflected light presents inverted (upside-down) and reversed (left to right), but with color and perspective intact.[fig3-7] It was commonly used as a drawing aid from the 16C on in the work of Vermeer and other masters of Western painting.[15] Daguerre used a camera obscura in his work at the Paris Opera House to paint panoramic mise-en-scène.

But what is relevant to our discussion is the impact that the arrival of photography had on the occupations of painters. Today, we imagine a painter as synonymous with an "artist," an elevated person expressing their inner creativity. But at the time of photography's arrival, painters were craftsmen, faithfully draughting pictures to order. 19C Europe was a time of profound social change, and being able to afford to have one's portrait made by a renowned painter, or having one of the era's great allegorical landscapes on one's sitting room wall, was a symbol that one had arrived in high society. Art schools were for training skilled

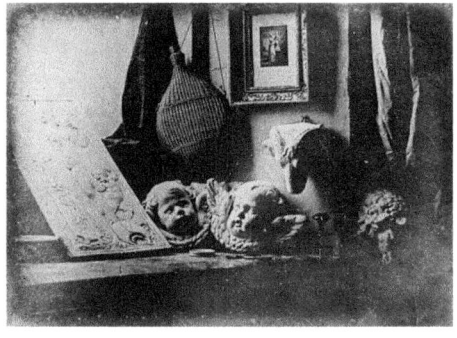

[fig3-6] *L'Atelier de l'artiste* (1837) One of the earliest examples of Daguerreotype photography.

[fig3-7] Camera Obscura

[fig3-8] Caricature of a portrait painter losing his trade to a photographer. (1843)

draughtsmen. Authorship was secondary to the details of the client's commission.

"À partir d'aujourd'hui, la peinture est morte" (From today, painting is dead)

The year is 1839, the year the daguerreotype was invented, and the sense of crisis is vividly reflected in the words of the painter Paul Delaroche,[16] who had just witnessed its demonstration. By 1840 there were already 10 or more photo studios in operation in Paris. By 1850, there were some 50, and by 1870, over 400. The fee at that time was about one week's wage for city workers. It's difficult to get a sense of whether this was expensive or cheap from a contemporary perspective, but it was unquestionably cheaper than commissioning a painter. The portrait artist, who would have invested decades in honing their craft, had become a caricature of themselves.[fig3-8]

Lithographic postcards of landscape paintings were popular

souvenirs from Europe's leading tourist destinations. By 1850, daguerreotype photographs had eviscerated the lithograph market in an early example of media jobs lost to automation. At the time, it was seen as comparable to the weavers of Luddite England, where an entire industry of craftspersons had been replaced by automation.

Today we consider painting as an art form with many styles, from hyper-realistic to abstracts specifically devoid of signifiers of any kind. But we have to remember that Paul Cézanne was only born in the same year that Daguerre invented photography. Modern art didn't exist yet. The Enlightenment and the French Revolution had introduced some liberty and religious tolerance, but there was another century of revolution and "disruption" to come. The *nouveau riche* were busy learning the classics, and the scientific method. The painting they wanted was realistic portraiture with enough glamorous embellishment to let their peers know that they too had arrived in the bourgeoisie. A painter had previously been valued as a draughtsman, primarily hired to replicate with precision. But the camera was far superior. No competition.

As the early modernist James McNeill Whistler[fig3-9] wrote, "The imitator is a pitiful creature. If the artist is only one who paints the appearance of trees, flowers and other things in front of him, then the king of artists would be a photographer. The artist's work should reflect something beyond that." Vincent Van Gogh echoed his statement: "What Pissarro says is true: You must boldly exaggerate the effects either of harmony or discord which colors produce; exact drawing, exact color, is not the essential thing because the reflection of reality in a mirror, if it could be caught, color and all, would not be a picture at all, no better than a photograph."

As cameras became more widespread, painters were freed from depicting the thing as is, and the skill became which subject to examine, and how, including exposition within the pictorial plane, and how the artist was reflected in doing so. Impressionism and tonalism emerged. It must have been a difficult time for many, but in retrospect, we see that the painters like Cézanne, and James McNeill Whistler rose within this crisis. We see the influence of photography in objects protruding from the frame, and heads being unceremoniously cropped off.[fig3-10] Caillebotte painted with a wide-angle lens.[fig3-11] In contrast to contemporary art from the 20th century onward, the painters of this era, such as Manet and Degas, were cutting-edge technologists, actively incorporating photographic grammar into their work. This is only possible because photography was proving more than just a means of replacing what painting had been. Rather, it was a voracious means of documentation. The visual world was being mapped, including phenomena, which humanity had always seen, but never fully understood.

Englishman Eadweard Muybridge (born Edward Muggeridge, in 1830 England) went to America and embarked on a number of careers. He was a bookseller, a photographic printer, a clothes washer innovator, a miner, and a banker. Yet after a traffic accident, which he survived,

[fig3-09] James McNeill Whistler, *Nocturne: Blue and Gold - Old Battersea Bridge* (1872–1875)

[fig3-10] Edgar Degas, *Singer of Cafe Console* (1878)

[fig3-11] Gustave Caillebotte, *European Bridge* (1876)

[fig3-12] Photographs of *Occident* in motion by Edward Muybridge. (1878)

but with a damaged frontal cortex, he was transformed. His hair turned white, and he became an artist. He converted his one-horse carriage into a portable darkroom and traveled the American West documenting the landscapes and architecture. Known for the "mathematical accuracy" of his work, Muybridge dabbled in an early version of time-lapse photography and made a profitable business in stereographic postcards. In 1972, rail magnate and then Californian governor Leland Stanford hired him to document his prize-winning racehorse Occident. No human had ever satisfactorily explained equine locomotion — people thought that they should logically trot with one foot anchoring them on the ground, or gallop like a dog with two front legs extended and then two rear legs extended. Stanford put the problem to Muybridge, leading to a series of studies, starting in 1873 and returning to the subject numerous times. In 1878, he innovated a battery of 12 cameras with shutters attached to trip-wires strung along the racetrack at Stanford's Palo Alto stock farm (now the Stanford University campus) and created a sequential series of photographs that definitively proved the phenomenon.[fig3-12] Muybridge also invented the zoopraxiscope, a cinema precursor, to present this series. The anime-inspired film *The Matrix* used this zoopraxiscope

[fig3-13]
Chronophotography by Etienne-Jule Marey (1890)

[fig3-14]
Marcel Duchamp
Nu descendant un escalier n° 2
(Nude Descending a Staircase, No. 2, 1912)

technique to shoot their "bullet time" special effects, showing that the technique still remains relevant even in the 21st century.

In parallel, in 1869, across the Atlantic, French cardiologist and inventor Étienne-Jules Marey had been constructing delicate artificial insects and fixing gold foil onto actual insect wings to study how they fly. He used soot-covered glass-fiber trip-wires to determine the insect's stroke order in the figure-8 shapes they produced in flight. He developed this fascination into a study of birds and adopted chrono-photography in the 1880s, using a gun-barrel-shaped photographic instrument to record several phases of movement on a single photographic surface, and published his findings in *Le Vol des Oiseaux* (The Flight of Birds) in 1890. His studies of humans in motion, in *Le Mouvement* (1894), show the functioning of human skeletal joint movements.[fig3-13]

Duchamp, the inventor of (selected modified ordinary manufactured objects) "readymades," such as the previously mentioned *Fountain*, owned a copy of *Le Mouvement*. And particularly in the 1911~1912 period, his paintings reflect this interest, as demonstrated in *Nu [esquisse], jeune homme triste dans un train* (Nude (Study), Sad Young Man on a Train) and *Nu descendant un escalier n° 2* (Nude Descending a Staircase, No. 2).[fig3-14] In both the former, in which the movement of the train and the movement of the subject in the train overlap, and in the latter, in which the movement of the body down the stairs is depicted like the movement of the skeleton and joints, the direct influence of Marey's studies is evident.

Impressionist paintings similarly deviate from the world-as-is, or as-was, to express a new post-photographic pictorial awareness; in breaking with former attempts at direct depiction to instead use detailed brush strokes to emphasize a more visceral sense of minute and constant

[fig3-15]
Works based on Dora Maar
Above: Man Ray, *Dora Maar* (1936)
Left: Pablo Picasso, *Portrait of Dora Maar* (1937)
Right: Michael McNaughton, *Portrait of Dora Maar* (2013)

changes in light, in their use of motion within the subject, and in their new senses of angle and composition.

The barriers to entry in the new world of photography were acceptably low, and many portrait painters who had lost their jobs soon began to introduce photography into their work. By the 1890s, continuing the tradition of making a portrait subject sit throughout the production process was described by British painter Walter Sickert as "nothing short of sadism."[17] Famous paintings thereafter were often based specifically on photographs because, in fact, it was always the painters' trained "eye" that they had been selling.

The two pictures and one photo on the previous page, each of a distinctive representation of the same person, symbolize painting, freed from realism by photographic technology, and emphasize the plasticity of image.[fig3-15] All three are of photographer, painter, and poet Dora Maar, perhaps best known as the inspiration and model for the famous Picasso paintings *Weeping Woman* and *Portrait of Dora Maar* (both 1937). In Man Ray's depiction, the area around her face has been polarized, and a small set of hands complements her own. We can see that in the first two, from masters of the 1930s, the effort was still to emphasize the expressive differences between painting and photography. The third, from 2013, is a color reproduction of a black-and-white portrait. Once photography became the norm, the act of manually drawing a photorealistic image began to have a different meaning and value.

Contrary to Delaroche's trepidations, the camera, and photographic technology's automation of image production opened entire new worlds of pictorial expression. The reason is that when humans are challenged by machines, they rise to produce new meanings. The same goes for musicians encountering computer-generated super-human dance rhythms, or beatboxing to reproduce those same drum machine sounds with their mouths.

3.5 The painter whose art was a mirror he himself was inside

The memetic imperative to self-replicate

The painter Harold Cohen was born in England in 1928 and studied painting at the Slade School of Fine Arts in London, where he also taught, as well as positions in various other faculties.[18] He represented Britain at the 1966 Venice Biennale, together with his brother Bernard, Anthony Caro, Robyn Denny, and Richard Smith, as one of *the British Five*. He also presented work in Documenta 3, the Paris Biennale, the Carnegie International and many other prestigious international shows. In 1968, Cohen joined the Visual Arts Department at UC San Diego, and thereafter remained in the Californian university system until the end of his career.

The tale is told in Pamela McCorduck's *AARON's Code: Meta-Art, Artificial Intelligence, and the Work of Harold Cohen* of a European art critic visiting the San Francisco Museum of Modern Art in 1979 while it was still installing an upcoming exhibition and noticing a large mural on the wall. The critic asks a nearby docent about the author of the work, stating that it reminded him of a Harold Cohen, but he wasn't familiar with Cohen's recent output. The docent replies that the painting was drawn by a computer, though the name Harold Cohen did sound familiar. Perhaps that might have been the programmer's name?

[fig3-16]
Cohen and *AARON* (1995)

When Cohen came to San Diego in 1968, he met a student with a passion for music and a master's degree in computer science. Cohen himself started programming for the first time at the age of 40, under the instruction of then UCSD graduate student Jeff Raskin, who later became the leader of the Macintosh development team at Apple. (The name Macintosh is after Ruskin's favorite varietal.) In 1971, Cohen took up a post as visiting scholar in the AI Laboratory at Stanford University and began developing a computer program called *AARON*,[19] in which he sought to codify the act of drawing.[fig3-16] After that, he devoted his time to developing *AARON*, one of the earliest examples of using AI to create art.[20] Cohen was fond of saying that he was going to be "the first artist who could have a posthumous show of new work." Why, at the height of his painting career, did he start? He described it as an attempt to redefine what a work of art can be.

It is important to understand that *AARON* is from an earlier era of AI. Computer programming is originally about breaking down decision-making into a series of conditional if-then-else branches, and Cohen realized that the artist's production process similarly has a series of aesthetic evaluations of the work in progress and conditional decision-making branches within it. He therefore began seeking ways to incorporate that process into an AI system. The algorithms behind *AARON* are not statistical analysis based on sample data, but rather huge chains of conditional branches hand-coded by Cohen himself.[21] *AARON* is procedural AI based on predetermined rules.

One example of Cohen's conditional branches is described in an interview: "You can read from the code that the direction of the upper arm according to the posture of the left hand is specified by the conditional branch if (left-arm-posture is "hand-on-hip") then (add-upper-arm left -.3 .5 .65) then (left-arm-posture is "arms-folded")..."[22]

These conditional branches literally replicate Cohen's own decision-making process, like DNA polymerases working in pairs to duplicate two identical DNA strands from one original DNA molecule in the process of genetic replication. *AARON* remembers all the lines he has drawn and stops when the specified certain conditions for a painting have been met. *AARON* is unique in that both the creation of the work and the feedback of the evaluation of the work being created are implemented within the same system. And this is essential because it clarifies that Cohen's interest was not in making a painting AI robot, but rather to clarify, formulate, and literally codify, his own artistic method. Coding was a rigorous and reliable means of proofing his own artistic method. He was creating a "meta" artwork to create art. For Cohen, *AARON* is at once a computer program for generating paintings, and at the same time a means of gaining a better understanding of his creative process in order to generate new insights into his own creative activities via paintings. Each new painting *AARON* produces demonstrates that Cohen's artistic process is sound. His search was primarily to identify the essence of what remains after mechanization. His work shows that to program in order to make a machine that imitates human creativity is, at its essence, an act of artistic creation. If "*art exists to signify that meaning is possible*" (from de Duve's *Kant After Duchamp*), then humans made computers to prove that thinking was possible.[23] AI was made to automate that process. When we think of computer art of the 1970s, we usually imagine orderly algorithmic beauty and complexity. In comparison, the heterogeneity of *AARON*'s clumsy meandering stands out.[fig3-17] *AARON*'s output more closely resembles cave paintings. Cohen spoke of *AARON* as a colleague. "I'm good at color, but *AARON* is top notch," Cohen laughs in an interview, saying that *AARON* often surprised Cohen himself.[fig3-18] "Using a computer to generate a visually attractive pattern is no different from using a camera to capture a landscape." But Cohen's intent was not that of a programmer expressing the beauty of mathematics to humans.[24] If learning is "imitation," then by creating the alter-ego algorithm *AARON*, Cohen was trying to learn the essence of art through drawing in a mirror. His journey was one of enormous purity, in the exploration of art via an abstract machine.

To summarize, AI is often described in terms of imitation, mimicry, a pale copy of human creativity; yet, the history of learning and creativity is itself a history of learning and mastery. Anthropomorphic verisimilitude necessarily creates a sense of anxiety and discomfort, and this is not limited to work in AI. The history of technological art, in photography and recording technology, is one of simultaneous repulsion and amazement to the public, and has upended entire creative industries. It has also spurred those creatives to greater and more noble heights, where many of our most beloved masterpieces sit.

It is important to note that the pursuit of replicating humans at anything is deeply flawed, and not because of the immaturity of the technology. Artists soon discovered new ways of making mistakes, and new vistas opened by technology which had little to do with what humans had previously done in those fields. Returning to the comments

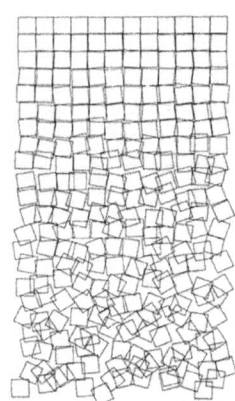
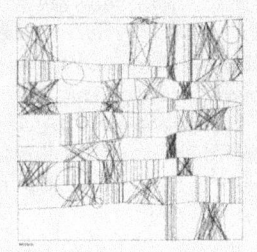
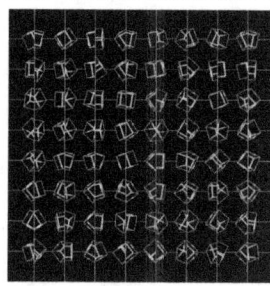

[fig3-17] Above: Abstract painting Early *AARON, Amsterdam Suite* F(1977)
Below: Other contemporaneous computer artworks
(from left to right)
Georg Nees, *Schotter* (1968)
Frieder Nake, *Hommage à Paul Klee, 13/9/65 Nr.2* (1965)
Manfred Mohr, *P-197* (1977)

[fig3-18]
Painting by late *AARON*,
Drawing (1987)

of Guardian critic Jones, the first thing many creatives do is learn how to "misuse" replication technology. Imitation, and failure to replicate, are indispensable creative acts. Even in biological evolutionary creation. We Homo Sapiens evolved due to natural replication errors, our attempts to replicate ourselves include unintended errors, and mutations in cultural genes created a wide variety of memetic "species."[25] The history of creation is a history of copying mistakes connecting from unicellular organisms to hip-hop. AI is but another phase.

"Those who do not want to imitate anything, produce nothing."

"Mistakes are almost always of a sacred nature. Never try to correct them. On the contrary: rationalize them, understand them thoroughly. After that, it will be possible for you to sublimate them." Salvador Dali[26]

The essence of imitation lies in the paradox of how each is necessarily incomplete, yet is able to trigger our cognitive mechanisms to recognize specific human traits in its forms and actions. The errors and heterogeneity which emerge from this gap are boundary explorations, learning opportunities. AI is, in a sense, neither imitation nor mimicry, but rather a mirror which reflects human actions by copying and externalizing them, so that we may better understand them.

Endnotes

1. This chapter is based on insights first encountered in the following books.
   Fumikazu Taniguchi, Katsushi Nakagawa, and Yudai Fukuda, *History of Acoustic Media* (Nakanishiya Publishing, 2015)
   Jonathan Sterne, *The audible past : cultural origins of sound reproduction* (Duke University Press, 2003)
2. Similar blind tests are being conducted between player pianos, which were popular in the 1910s and 20s, and live pianists.
   Hiroshi Watanabe, *The Birth of the Audience: Music Culture in the Post-Modern Era* (Chuokoron-Shinsha, 2012)
3. Berliner, Edison's rival and inventor of the disc-style gramophone, liked this painting and purchased it with the condition that he should replace the Edison-style gramophone originally drawn in the painting with Berliner's. Later, the picture was registered as a trademark as HMV, the acronym for His Master's Voice, a record shop that exists into the present day.
4. The words of John Philip Sousa, who is known for his compositions such as *The Stars and Stripes Forever*.
5. As a pioneering example, I would like to mention the efforts of Pierre Henry, Pierre Schaeffer and others in *musique concrète*.
6. George Martin, with Jeremy Hornsby, *All You Need Is Ears: The inside personal story of the genius who created The Beatles* (Macmillan, 1979)
   In the production of *Being for the Benefit of Mr. Kite* (included in the album *Sergeant Peppers Lonely Hearts Club Band*), tapes with old organ songs were randomly cut, thrown, collected, reconnected, and then played backwards to achieve the effect.
7. Antares Audio Technologies, *Auto-Tune*
   https://www.antarestech.com/
8. *Is AI Misora Hibari "blasphemy"? Let's Examine what pop icon Tatsuro Yamashita said with an AI researcher* (Asahi Shimbun Digital, 02.2020)
   https://www.asahi.com/articles/ASN1Z4FC8N1YUCVL025.html
9. John Walden, *Yamaha Vocaloid Leon & Lola*, Sound on Sound (2004)
   https://www.soundonsound.com/reviews/yamah-avocaloid-leon-lola
   According to the contemporaneous reviews, it was easy to make a robot voice, but trying to make a realistic singing voice was a daunting task.
10. The English language manual was nearly 100 pages long.
11. See the 2015 documentary film *808* (Alex Dunn, director)
12. Also from *808*, the words of Ikutaro Kakehashi.
13. Elias Leight, *8 Ways the 808 Drum Machine Changed Pop Music* (Rolling Stone, 12.2016)
    https://www.rollingstone.com/music/music-news/8-ways-the-808-drum-machine-changed-pop-music-249148/
14. The following materials form the starting points for discussions in this section:
    Aaron Scharf, *Art and Photography* (Penguin Books, 1983)
    Aaron Hertzmann, *Can Computers Create Art?* / Arts (2018)
15. As discussed in the film Tim's Vermeer (High Delft Pictures, 2014)
16. A French painter known for his realistic depictions of historical figures.
17. Sickert was rumored to be a culprit in a series of freakish murders attributed to Jack the Ripper.
18. Pamela McCorduck, *Aaron's Code: Meta-Art, Artificial Intelligence, and the Work of Harold Cohen* (W. H. Freeman & Co, 1990)
19. Cohen is quoted as intending to create a series of painting programs, and name them in alphabetical order, starting with Aaron, AA. Aaron is also Harold Cohen's Hebrew name.
20. Grant D. Taylor, *When the Machine Made Art: The Troubled History of Computer Art* (Bloomsbury Academic, 2014)
21. AARON was initially written in C, but later moved to the LISP language, which

makes it easier to write highly abstract expressions.
22 Christopher Scoates, *Brian Eno: Visual Music* (Chronicle Books, 2013)
23 Arthur C. Danto, *What Art Is* (Yale University Press, 2013)
24 Grant D. Taylor, *When the Machine Made Art: The Troubled History of Computer Art* (Bloomsbury Academic, 2014)
25 Alex Mesoudi, *Cultural Evolution: How Darwinian Theory Can Explain Human Culture and Synthesize the Social Sciences* (University of Chicago Press, 2011)
26 Jackie De Burca, *Salvador Dali at Home* (White Lion Publishing, 2018)
    Salvador Dalí, *Dali by Dali* (Abrams, 1970)

Chapter —— 4

AI Aesthetics— The impact of AI on expression

4.1 The Peacock's Tail—Optimization pitfalls

Harms of Allocation, Harms of Representation

At the beginning of this book, I wrote about how the first thing that an AI researcher learns is that the goalposts are moved after each goal. The danger of the constant moving of the goalposts is, of course, when objectivity is lost, and the discipline of the game changes. This is key to AI because, at heart, AI automation is based on the ability to recognize and structure data. When AI works well, it can be almost prophetic in how it can reveal more than we anticipate.

ML models' utility can be evaluated by how well they can generalize and make useful predictions, a metric known as modeling fitness. By assessing whether a model is appropriately fit, underfit, or overfit, we can adjust accordingly, utilizing exposure to previously unseen data. Underfitting occurs where a data model fails to accurately capture the relationship between input and output variables. Overfitting happens when the model precisely fits the data provided, but struggles with unfamiliar (unseen) data. Achieving fitness involves dividing the ML model data into two sets—training data and evaluation data. Then, provide only the training data to the AI model, while withholding the evaluation data remains concealed, serving as a benchmark for progress. Evaluation data error results are not used in training data updates, because they could corrupt this blind. Like a classroom where students' comprehension is measured via textbook review at mid-term and applied questions in the finals, the combination provides a learning refinement structure. A situation in which good grades are obtained for training data but only bad results are obtained for unknown data is called "overfitting," serving as proof that the solution is not generalized enough. Like a student who has memorized the textbook answers and hasn't learned how to apply their knowledge. Underfitting and overfitting are both functions of data bias and variance. Bias means assumptions made by a model to make a function easier to learn. Variance means when you train your data and obtain a very low error, then change the data and experience a high rate of error. If your model is underfit, it has too much bias and too little variance. The relatively high bias keeps it from deriving rules, and therefore the output is too flexible and random. If your model is overfit, then it doesn't derive rules, but rather sticks to the specifics of your training data, warts and all. Overfitting is low bias — dogmatic adherence to the data set — and the output, therefore, reflects no larger lessons than precisely what is in the data set. But even a "fit" model can malfunction due to cultural biases in the datasets.

AI development was always subject to its inputs. AI technologies such as DL engage in unstructured learning and use volumes of data which are orders of magnitude larger. Language is originally a cultural inheritance built on the palimpsest bedrock of biases and inequalities from earlier human societies. Since the millennium, virtually all text, audio, and video have become fully digital, through the past 15 years of smartphone and Social Networking Systems (SNS) ubiquity, an unprecedented flood of personal data has been generated. Training data fed on data generated by the "engagement" algorithms at the heart of SNS is just as likely to be doom-scrolling emotional teenagers as it is to be a "rational actor" citizenry. As most of us know, a certain level of critical thinking and fact-checking among a rational distribution of sources is advisable when taking information from the Internet. AI isn't yet capable of critical thinking, so the job of checking data sources and bias contained in the ML models is a tremendous challenge to create greater equity in our societies going forward.

Writer, musician, and academic Dr. Kate Crawford has proposed a useful framework for algorithmic feature detection or classification bias according to the type of harm caused: *Harms of Allocation*, which refers to resulting misallocations of opportunities or resources, and *Harms of Representation*, which refer to reinforced prejudices and stereotypes.[1] *Harms of Allocation* are system failures which occur when resources become bottlenecked or otherwise inappropriately allocated as the result of a dataset. Examples include automated eligibility systems, ranking algorithms, and predictive risk models. Consider financial institutions' attempts to introduce AI-based systems to improve prospective customers' creditworthiness.

According to the Brookings Institution, in 2016, the net worth of a typical white family is $171,000, nearly ten times greater than that of the $17,150 for a typical Black family. Based just on that information alone, a bank's credit score AI training data would weigh 10-to-1 towards typical white customers, and in doing so contribute to further

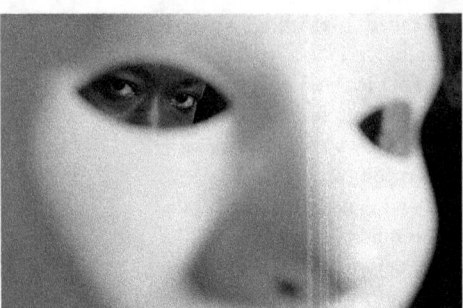

[fig4-1]
Joy Buoramwini gazing through a white mask.

entrenching asset inequality. We in Japan aren't multi-racial enough for that to be our litmus, but it's easy enough to switch the focus to gender bias, credit score viability of men vs. women, and find similar patterns of systemic misallocation.

Harms of Representation are arguably more relevant to our discussion of AI and creativity. These failures occur when AI models reduce participatory and expressive affordance. MIT Media Lab-based digital activist and creator Joy Buolamwini works to identify bias against underrepresented groups in code and develop practices for accountability during their design. Dr. Buolamwini was working on an AI artwork called the *Aspire Mirror*, which used facial recognition algorithms to reflect aspirational others. She anticipated that it would reflect someone she aspired to, with a similar skin type, like Serena Williams, but instead found that the technology couldn't even recognize her, much less express her ideals. Her journey to explore such harms of representation led to her artwork *The Coded Gaze*, a documentary short film of her needing to don a white mask to be recognized by the computer, then removing it, and being unable to be "seen," therein highlighting the potential for bias in AI facial recognition.[fig4-1] Dr. Buolamwini's research further explores how AI patterns racial and gender biases, underperforming for Blacks and Asians, reflecting the technology's development by North American and European heterosexual "pale male" Caucasian men.[2]

Facial recognition systems have been introduced to prevent fraud in online exams in the United States. Online American bar association examinations require the camera to be on and facial recognition active at all times. Darker-skinned participants are forced to prepare special light which shines directly into their faces throughout the two-day test for the systems to function.[3]

StyleGAN is a GAN framework (referred to in Chapter 2) whose purpose is to synthesize artificial examples, such as pictures, and is commonly used to create convincing photorealistic fake human face portraits. The PULSE framework was a single-image super-resolution

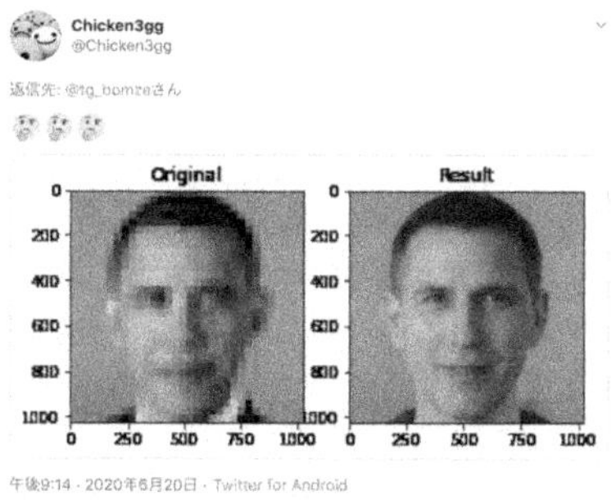

[fig4-2]
Results from a model that upscales low-resolution images.

StyleGAN model to construct high-resolution images from low-resolution input.[4] One of the most famous incidences of training data bias, or arguably Harms of Representation, occurred when a Twitter user entered a low-resolution photo of former U.S. President Obama, and the StyleGAN produced a high-resolution image of a Caucasian President. [fig4-2] Even next-generation StyleGAN2 architecture continues to generate Caucasian faces at a rate of 70% or more.[5]

The ability to generate target-group-attractive copyright-free models is obviously profitable for advertisers. Dating app companies have also found StyleGANs effective for creating fake accounts/advertising, meaning that, at whatever level, there may be some impact on perceived evolutionary fitness. Japan is not a multiracial society, yet caucasian-featured models have long reflected Japanese cultural bias in advertising (making up more than 72% of all non-East Asian models, according to a 2003 survey[6]).

Even in anime and manga, cultural expressions primarily associated with Japan, figures are typically abstracted to make them look less racially Japanese, or East Asian. This was generally considered a non-issue until recently, when a manga caricature of Haitian-Japanese tennis superstar Naomi Osaka appeared in a Nissin noodle advertisement and was criticized internationally as a case of "whitewashing."[7] Most Japanese probably identified the depiction of Ms. Osaka as in the mode of *The Prince of Tennis* manga franchise, a Seishun Academy tennis team member, all of whom are pale skinned, less "East Asian" looking Japanese (*the Prince of Tennis* author Takeshi Konomi was commissioned to produce the commercial). Nissin stated that they were embarrassed to have not been respectful of international norms, saying, "We accept that we are not sensitive enough and will pay more attention to diversity issues in the future."

Fitness & Aesthetics

What about how filters in Snapchat, Instagram, and Facetune, which studies have shown exacerbate Body Dysmorphic Disorder (BDD) in teens? According to a blistering report in the Wall Street Journal in September 2021, Instagram makes body image issues worse for "one in three teenage girls," and "Teens blame Instagram for increases in the rate of anxiety and depression," according to internal Facebook research, and that "This reaction was unprompted and consistent across all groups."

Of course, the Harms are not just self-identification. With the popularization of camera-equipped smartphones bundled with simple AI value-added photo processing software, and popular platforms such as Instagram and Snapchat, we find the dual phenomenon of exponentially more people of all ages making photographic contributions, and AI camera features increasingly pre-selecting and recommending what is a good photograph. It's one thing when these features are simply aiding quantitative indicators such as available brightness and contrast, but with image modification filters, for example, aesthetic criteria are also defined. In 2018, Huawei Technologies Co., Ltd. held a photo contest entirely based on their AI-based in-camera photo evaluation mechanism,[8] where AI was the judge and jury.

Most of the sample data sets used in ML in music, for example, are based on Western classical and pop music. If we compare the datasets for machine training published by ISMIR, an international society for music information processing, 125 datasets are related to Western music, while a mere 14 data sets are non-Western.[9] If the entire discourse about music is defined within Western parameters, it must be a pretty myopic discussion. Lev Manovich has been particularly brilliant about the cultural harms in media technology, describing the relationship between aesthetic and cultural transformations in his essay *AI Aesthetics*. Manovich points out that the biggest concern in AI aesthetics is how systems tend to automate our processes of aesthetic creation and choice, leading to a spiraling cultural reductionism.

One of the clearest examples of such self-reinforcing reductionism can be found in the record industry, as playlists become datasets to be mined for metadata to create new songs. Now that audio-visual electronic entertainment is becoming typically rented rather than owned, streamed rather than played, each point of consumption generates metadata, with streaming service providers feeding music labels detailed data about which songs are being listened to by how many people at what time in great detail. According to an article in Japan's Nikkei economic daily, streaming services provide music labels with detailed data about which songs are listened to, by whom, and how many, including timestamps, artist name, and song title, as well as genre, tempo, and volume.[10] Reviewing the API specs for Spotify developers, we additionally find mood, danceability, and instrumentation, including acoustic or electric, and the presence or absence of vocals. Sales data has been analyzed since the days of 1950s radio play, but the amount and granularity of data available now is essentially incomparable. Popular producers often work from this metadata. According to the same Nikkei article, artists, genres, tempos, and tones are used to generate streaming targets from production. Record company releases are investments, and the expected ROI per element of each song can be assessed in more-or-less real-time. As this trend accelerates, we can expect increased pressures to produce according to data optimization. Such overfitting culture might also threaten the creative health of both consumers and producers.

Popular culture, by definition, already had this tendency. Think of the song *Blurred Lines* by Robin Thicke, described as a case of a client pursuing a groove over-inspired by Marvin Gaye's *Got to Give it Up*, too timid about innovating from the original, too satisfied to draw within the original lines. Everyone who's ever worked in commercial creative acts, or created themselves, knows the danger of mimicking past success too closely, and that's what most clients will typically request. A smart metadata-trained AI could easily generate 1,000 versions of near *Blurred Lines*, none of which actually reference the original innovations or charm of *Got to Give it Up*, and thereby each would serve to dilute the point of each other's existence, and maybe even vanquish the original like a self-negating *Library of Babel*. This begs the question, what is fair game? After all, Olivia Rodrigo, hit songstress of 2021, sparked numerous online discussions about how overfit her creative output is, in directly referencing her creative input. Most of Led Zeppelin's first three albums directly reference readily identifiable sources. How do we quantify innovation within these memetic lulls, reinforced as they are by profit-seeking incentives?

Harms of Overfitting

The spectacular example of overfitting in the animal world is the peacock's tail feathers which, dazzling and entertaining as they may be, with their convolutional neural network-like patterning and size, profoundly troubled Darwin. Their plumage suggested an example of the struggle to leave more offspring than their competitors being achieved at the cost of racing towards an evolutionary dead-end. If, in the absence of predation, the peacock's evolution is accelerated by a single factor, in this case the peahen's preference for long tails. The peacock's tail has become the classic example of aesthetics crippling performance; what population geneticist R.A. Fisher calls "runaway selection." Males with shorter tails should normally be better adapted to flight, and escape. Absent the natural correction mechanism of predation, each generation of males exhibits longer tails, and each generation of peahens continues to exhibit a preference for longest among them.

Just like the peacock's tail, accelerating bias in AI training data tends to strengthen existing evaluation regimes and drive us away from fitness. We would like to think of evolution as a process of optimization, weeding out overfitting and underfitting, that we human beings are the natural victors at the forefront of intelligence and evolution. And yet, imagine the "winner's circle" if all animals similarly "succeeded" and gained Homo sapiens qualities. Such an ecosystem would have dangerously little diversity, and be dangerously fragile. Evolution is a process of diversification, risk re-distributions. Optimization is necessarily relative to what may potentially be needed to survive, and not what was previously needed to survive. But there are baselines: The plant on my desk comes from a natural intelligence evolution incomparably longer than my dog's. Each drive toward optimization comes with risks of diversity loss. The more we use AI for creative and expressive activities, the more important it is to protect cultural diversity, and to nurture alternative intelligences. To constantly re-examine where value is created. And how creative endeavors should be defined, and modeled for the next generation?

4.2 Sinatra doo be doo be no do no K-POP

The dis-embodiment

In April 2020, OpenAI announced Jukebox,[11] and opened a new era of AI music generation, subverting conventional wisdom about the rules of the game, to general delight and dismay. Jukebox's menu is simple: the user selects a singer from a list of some of the Western world's most popular artists, song lyrics, and a genre. Jukebox AI then generates a song, whole cloth. I say "whole cloth" because Jukebox generates no MIDI data, no sheet music, no procedural analytical mechanisms. Jukebox AI can re-produce musical facsimiles hierarchically, from training data of 1.2 million famous artists, lyrics, and genres. You can provide the lyrics, but otherwise entire songs, including all elements, such as vocals, melody, rhythm, and instrumentation, are directly generated as raw audio waveforms. Keys, chords, notes, and rhythms, have not been explicitly modeled. Western 12-tone music theory has not been modeled. Everything "learned" is from memorizing patterns in raw audio waveforms, and finished "music," such as one might hear on a CD or streaming service, is produced directly. If the Dadabots is a *Relentless Doppelganger* chimera freak show, then Jukebox is like the Great Pacific Garbage Patch of every popular song ever misheard. Deep fakes, using singer's names, music genres, and lyrics: entire song approximations generated "by" those "singers'" voices.

Previous experiments with generating directly from raw audio waveforms had not produced meaningful output, due to the complexity of the context and the volume of computation. Previous experiments with generating directly from raw audio waveforms had not produced meaningful output, due to the complexity of the context and the volume of computation. Enter deep-pocketed OpenAI, to leapfrog this problem with smart VQ-VAE (Vector-Quantized Variational Auto-Encoder) algorithms, and capital at unprecedented volumes and speeds. OpenAI was able to model the data of 1.2 million songs by running 512 GPUs for 6 weeks, or over $5+ million in dollars for the hardware alone, not to mention electricity costs.[12] To the computers, of course, it was not music, or artists, but rather wholesale number-crunching: they might as well have been minting cryptocurrency. Jukebox is a mechanism for learning complex relationships within recorded waveform patterns on records and CDs, and building a huge model from that. There is no musical structure analysis per se, so the fact that we perceive the reproduced waveform patterns as music, and identifiable artists, is a function of our cultural conditioning. Their re-creation (?) or, rather, ability to stimulate our recognition of, a "Ye" singing "Elvis" in a hip-hop style, or a "Bob Marley" covering "Dylan-esques," or whatever we should call that output, is a truly impressive feat of computation. The technological advancement that Jukebox represented, in professional-quality 44kHz audio, opened whole new questions in cognitive science; it heralded a new phase in the evolution of "deepfake" music. I'm sure that the entire project was surely in violation of the copyrights of each of its many authors and performers. None of the artists affiliated with those 1.2 million songs in the training data participated with consent, any more than Misora Hibari participated in *Kohaku* 2019.

Jukebox released their model weights, training, and sampling code, so I immediately tried it. It took nearly a whole day to generate a 30-second snippet, even with my high-end if admittedly still consumer-level GPU, so it's clearly not something that everyone will be able to experiment with just yet. My first attempt using their model was to generate *Somewhere Over the Rainbow* by "Frank Sinatra" in the style of "Classic Rock." Each started with Vegas-style audience banter before the actual track began and audience applause during the interlude—very heyday Rat Pack, and rather unexpected. Each time I generated a new version, even under the exact same parameters, slightly different versions were generated: One a bit jazzier, another with more of a Latin touch. Of course, no two versions will ever be the same, because none of them exist before being generated. There were noise artifacts, which I initially found annoying, before realizing that they were also just verisimilitude to the live recordings of that era used in the training data. It isn't "music," it's just recognizably "musical" patterns. But what does this say about authorship? They certainly weren't my compositions. Were they "written" by (*Somewhere Over the Rainbow* authors) Harold Arlen and Yip Harburg? Frank Sinatra? OpenAI? My first guess would be that this is just like the episode with Obvious, obfuscating the role of AI artist Robbie Barrat, who devised the GAN algorithm that generated those bourgeois portraits. But what complicates the question in this case is that their invention isn't musical, it's mathematical. Effectively, zero humans would be able to recognize it in printed form. So it's hard to say that a given researcher or engineer intended to do one thing or another musically. But that's what separates it from its predecessors. The results are far too derivative, entirely constructed directly from the work of artists in the sample data, and our ability to recognize the output as such, to say that Jukebox itself created the songs.

My conclusion was that the authors of the "Sinatra" simulacra generated on my system are the OpenAI researchers who created the Jukebox instrument which generated it, though the essence of the Jukebox instrument's "creativity" resides in its training data. My reasoning is that, because Jukebox produces black-box output, absent MIDI, sheet music, or any other form of music structural analysis, each song generation is a singular performance. No engineer could claim to have intended the results I achieved with any level of specificity. Jukebox's character is distinct from previous AI music generation technology. I tested this thesis by attempting to generate "Sinatra" doing "Justin Bieber" in a "J-Pop" style, and the results were DOA. There are simply too few cultural pathways between the genres. Without common reference points in the cultural inheritance of the data, nothing identifiably "musical" was generated, in my sense of recognition of what is music, at least. Perhaps Jukebox is primarily interested in the unmistakable new levels of ambiguity about authorship that it proposes?

So how would this be taken to market? What if I created a "Sinatra"-based "hip-hop" mash-up, with original lyrics, and donated the proceeds to charity?[13] In this case, the intention and lyrics would be mine, but would the Sinatra estate, or the rights holders of the work that was in the 1.2 million songs of training data, feel that their contributions were recognized, much less compensated? What if I performed a Sinatra impersonation over a backing track? Or, if I did a DJ remix, integrating actual Sinatra, and hip-hop, to original lyrics? It seems clear that AI only further complicates the already thorny questions of authorship in the collective consciousness, if not legal precedent of music rights stewardship. Of course, it's not ready for market, nor will anyone likely bring it to market immediately. The sound quality is still, honestly, unsatisfactory. And nothing I've heard generated yet has seemed finished enough to chart. On the other hand, it's a fast-moving field, and Jukebox will improve. A coherent and moving Jukebox song is only x number of experiments away. It can't be long until a wellspring of cohesive listenable songs can be generated at the touch of a button. A new Beatles album? No. But chartable music? What's to stop it? And when that happens, who will be the author?

AI-generated songs on the market will naturally be weeded out by listeners' tastes, you might say. On platforms like Spotify and YouTube, the metadata being collected, not only the listener's personal attribute information (age, gender, place of residence, favorite artist, favorite sport / movie / game…), but also where and where the music was skipped are recorded. Detailed information about playback, such as who listened how far to each track, is collected. Who recommended this channel to them, or who would be likely to be influenced by them to listen to it? Increasingly optimized AI models will hone in on tunes and styles more perfectly tailored to listener tastes. The AI-generated songs generated in this way will then, in turn, be used as training data for the next generation of AI music models. This kind of pattern identification and acceleration is exactly what AI is good at. Of course, it's not just limited to music. Consumer data has driven markets since people learned to aggregate it. And AI is just a form of statistical analysis working at a scale producing effects that still seems novel to us. If we don't learn to use it appropriately, it will simply overfit our aesthetics into vortexes of peacock's-tailed irrelevance. Not limited to music, of course, AI can be generally regarded as a mechanism, which participates behind the scenes through learning from information generated by ordinary consumers. One might argue that audience tastes have always been created from the social *milieu*, and that every artist today carries the influence of artists like Sinatra or Dylan. My point is that current AI-based music generation systems are making this feedback process more immediate and explicit, and capable of mutating faster than we may be able to recognize.[fig4-3]

Who would listen to AI music?, you might ask yourself, but the answer is, of course, you, without even realizing it. In March 2019, Endel became the "first-ever algorithm to sign [a]major label deal," as Warner Music approached them with a distribution deal for 600 tracks on 20 albums that were then put on streaming services, returning a 50 / 50 royalty split.[14] Anybody on social media has probably already heard some. Music streaming platforms including Spotify have introduced playlist-based viewing styles, replacing traditional album-based music viewing, and that's an opportunity for algorithmic generics. The most popular playlists on Spotify are, not coincidentally, music that helps you concentrate, like work-outs, and music that will put you to sleep.[15] Music that is anonymous is preferential for resting, and can also be optimized for better sleep based on brain science and clinical trials.[16] Both make it ideal for AI. And for the labels, the music keeps playing while you sleep, generating more plays through the night, and higher copyright royalty returns. (Interestingly, in 2019, when Billie Eilish released *when we all fall asleep where do we go,* her fans responded by making her the #1 artist for streams between 01:00~06:00 am., demonstrating that artists can hack metadata too!)

Consider *Authors Guild v Google* (court case, 2003-2015) and Google's stated mission "to organize the world's information and make it universally accessible and useful." Google's mission to create a digital dataset of the world's printed knowledge and make it available, and searchable put them in direct conflict with the previous regime of authors' rights agreements. The Authors Guild argued that Google was making access to the books available in order to increase advertising revenue. Google understood that, in the *Library of Babel* that is AI, search is creation. They argued that, in the name of making the entirety of print available, they were aggregating an unprecedented set of one of the largest bodies of human knowledge online. Core reference texts

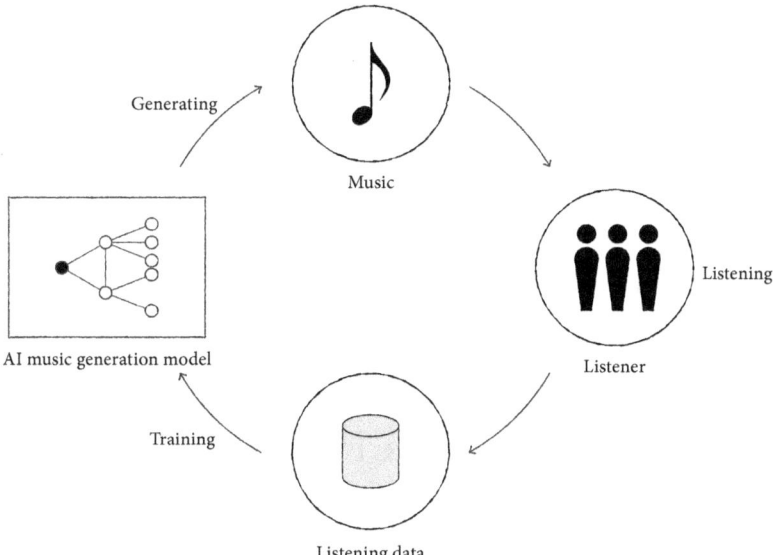

[fig4-3]
Relationship between AI music generation model and listener.

should be especially important, especially as we approach a world where AI will be able to generate an entire Library of Babel nominally equivalent to any song, book, or other copyrighted work, without attributable copyright. Of course, Google wasn't releasing an AI model which could do this in print. But Jukebox can arguably do that in music.

Once again, we can see how AI melts our ideals of authorship and harvests our collective inheritance. As a DJ, this seems like familiar territory. DJs are understood as curators and instigators, resuscitating careers, and reinvigorating composers with their playlists, and are often co-credited and compensated as such. Our creative contributions similarly have a multi-layered structure, as do, increasingly, music producers. Composition may also be regarded as a multi-layered creative act in which more actors are intertwined by utilizing AI.

4.3 "Seeds" over "artifacts" — The dissolution of fixed "works"

Economic historian Eckhard Höffner compares how Great Britain adopted copyright law in 1710, and the largest German state, Prussia, only from 1837. Höffner tells of how English publishers' business models were built on exploiting exclusive publication rights, typically printing no more than 750 copies, often at a price exceeding the weekly salary of an educated worker. Their model was built on first editions. Book buyers were wealthy aristocrats, and books were equated with elements of luxury. It was common that the most valuable leather-bound illustrated volumes would be bolted to shelves by chains to protect against thieves. At the same time, Germany's continued division into small states meant that it was hardly possible to enforce the law throughout the empire until the unification of Germany in 1918. This lack of copyright in Germany, and uneven copyright laws among states, meant that any number of authentic or spurious versions of any text could be produced cheaply. In 1843, German publishers published about 14,000 new books, most of which were scientific publications, which accounting for population, is roughly the same as what is published today. For comparison, only about 1,000 new works were published in Great Britain that year. Höffner's thesis is that the lack of copyright actually contributed to the technological revolution in Germany in the 19th century. The introduction of Prussian copyright, and the nature of how those rights were framed around the Rights of the Author created a much larger *Library of Babel* in pre-unification Germany. In England, the copyright regime was developed around the upper classes, and so literature, philosophy, theology, philology, and historiography, which were important for the classical education system to be developed. This also meant that publishers could produce editions to the extent that authors permitted, which meant that scientific papers, for example, came out in Germany in huge print runs at extremely low prices. Even the poor in provincial hamlets had access to books, and could develop libraries. This huge potential readership incentivized scientists to publish the results of their work. For example, Sigismund Hermbstädt, a German professor of chemistry, published a book on tissue bleaching in 1806 which earned him a greater fee than the English writer Mary Shelley did from her bestselling novel *Frankenstein*, which came out the same year. Commercially one sold en masse, the other sold in limited editions. According to Höffner, this new form of disseminating knowledge even replaced education at school or university to some extent. Memetically one remains with us as culture, and the other has been folded into the sum of scientific knowledge.

Japan modernized under duress, from the 1850s, under the threat of American nation-building. Fortunately, the Americans didn't keep their promise to colonize and returned to fight a civil war instead. But the threat they posed did wake Japan to the need to master colonial modernity before it mastered them. Japan built boats and sent scholars abroad, and one of the things they brought back was the Prussian legal framework, including the Moral Rights of the Author. The moral rights of an author work together with the property rights related to the fruits of their labor. The property rights can be sold, but even if sold, violations can be difficult to litigate if the author believes that the violation honors the work, in effect their good name, and the good name of the greater body of what they created. The result is that the Japanese pop culture industry is open-sourced across millions of consumer/producers, cosplayers, or *dojinshi* (unauthorized "subcultural" remix comics using, and commenting on, famous characters from major pop cultural canons) creators who create everything from sculptural, textual, and musical products from many globally famous Japanese pop franchises, and in the process encouraging enormous talent and a sense of ownership among the fanbase, and creating a highly media literate consumer/producer society. I say "open-sourced" because participants are generally both consumers and producers. Hypothetically, tens of "unauthorized" versions of, say, *Dragon Ball* comics will be created by fans of *Dragon Ball* and will be available at these conventions, and then enter very limited circulation. As long as Akira Toriyama, the original author of *Dragon Ball*, tacitly approves of the existence, and limited exploitation of these "unauthorized" versions, then no other rights holder can stop them from producing them. This has led to about 4 decades and millions of copies of "unauthorized" versions, some adding storylines that are then reflected in the official versions, or of story writers or draughtspersons, or inking specialists, etc. being able to present their talents and rising. It makes everything more like a blues culture, where Ray Charles can convert *It Must be Jesus* into *I Got a Woman*, and anybody can sit in on the session, and maybe show their "chops" in one way or another.

In America and the UK, of course, the intellectual property continued in the British model, and the result is that the American pop culture industry is dominated by a handful of colossal rights holders, such as Marvel, DC, Disney, and Hasbro, and each new license to exploit needs to be aware of infringing on the rights of all previous rights holders.

Mozart's *Requiem* is one of the most beloved compositions of all time, but it is also a product of this period of copyright contingency. Many elements already appear in the composer Michael (younger brother of Joseph) Haydn's *Requiem*, written twenty years earlier, and which Mozart is known to have seen performed many times. This does not to say that Mozart plagiarized, but rather to point out that our contemporary conception of authorship and copyright is also not fixed, and was different for musicians in other eras. And this is another reason why Mozart could publish his *Requiem* in 1791 while an effectively similar composition, Haydn's *Requiem*, had already been published in 1771. To put it another way, if Mozart and Haydn had published under British law, we might not ever have heard Mozart's *Requiem*. Due to the effects of 19C pre-unification Germany's copyright laws, we can reference both, exactly as they were written centuries ago. In that time, music functioned more as a shared property, a "standard" in today's vernacular, the composer less important than a given interpretation. At the time, music was an adjunct to social gatherings and religious events, so songs typically changed with each performance. From the time of the *Guttenberg Galaxy*, the identity of the music came to be recognized in association with the rights of the author, due to mass production via letterpress printing technology. Sheet music kept the identity of the music and facilitated distribution. This is the moment when the score became equated with music, property of an author.

This issue of copyright is problematized in AI. Recording technology made another level of song uniqueness possible. Each independent work, including not only the tone of each note, its articulation (pronunciation method), and acoustic engineering, including effects. But this was upended because of sampling law. From the beginning of hip-hop, and DJ culture, the perfect beats of George Clinton and Funkadelic were always a rich vein to be mined. However, years later, a copyright lawyer named Armen Boladian, and his company Bridgeport Music, who represented the rights of Clinton and Funkadelic, took many DJs to court. In the 2005 case of *Bridgeport Music v. Dimension Film*, the court ruled that samples consisting of as little as two seconds of recorded sound still constituted copyright violations, a ruling which effectively closed the mine, and made sampling inviable thereafter.

Berlin-based American composer, musician, and sound artist Holly Herndon holds a PhD from Stanford University's Center for Computer Research in Music and Acoustics. Pitchfork magazine acclaimed Herndon's "crystalline voice as a chief input for her laptop, ultimately arriving at a poignant nexus of electronic accessibility and experimentation that owes as much to her academic forebears as her club contemporaries. It's a record with the rare capacity to turn cynics who might scoff at the idea of laptops-as-intimate-instruments into believers." Herndon is exploring new frontiers of musical expression and vocal sovereignty by open sourcing a "vocal deepfake" SampleRNN trained on her own voice. Herndon's work with ML, and IP and vocal sovereignty, in Voice Modeling is pioneering both as an art form, and in laying the groundwork for discerning Voice Modeling IP provenance, which is essential work in a world of increasing deepfakes freely available on the Internet. Her 2019 album *PROTO* created as a collaboration between herself and her "AI baby" Spawn, truly broke new ground.

Sample-like sound sources became the only viable option for musicians working in these forms of music. Jean Baudrillard's simulacra, a condition in which only the "real" without origin or reality was possible — no longer a territory, but rather a referential being or a substance, generated by models. A future with AI playing a larger role in the creative process means not only the disappearance of identifiable authorship in some cases, and therefore a loss of whatever legal and compensatory protections copyright afforded, but increasingly even the idea of a work as a fixed, unique, and independent existence. As the Jukebox example shows, there may increasingly be innumerable variations of every "strain" of AI product, until the very concept of "work," as a thing which is fixed and exists independently, must also melt.

The dissolving boundary between sender and receiver

The artist who seems to have arrived preternaturally prepared for this condition is celebrated ambient music pioneer and "non-musician" Brian Eno, encapsulated in his thesis statement: "Ambient music must be able to accommodate many levels of listening attention without enforcing one in particular; it must be as ignorable as it is interesting." Known for his solo work, as well as collaborative productions with Roxy Music, David Bowie, Talking Heads, U2, and Coldplay, his *Generative Music 1* "album" was released on a floppy disc, on Windows PC software just as I was exploring my own future in music production.

Eno describes the concept of his generative music as follows:[17] "I was inspired initially by certain screensavers - those little graphic devices that use very little computer memory but keep generating new images on the screen. I wrote several proposals based on the idea of using the computer to make music in a similar manner - not as a way of replaying huge chunks of preformed material (which was what was being done, to devastatingly miserable effect, with CD-Roms at the time) but instead as a place where compositional "seeds" provided by the composer would be grown. I thought this made composing into a kind of genetic activity — in the sense that the compositional "seeds" were actually interacting sets of rules and parameters rather than precise musical descriptions. I imagined the piece evolving out of the interaction of these probabilistic rule-sets—and therefore evolving differently in each "performance."" "I

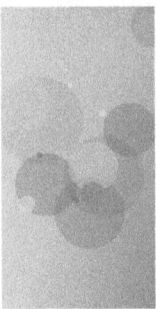

[fig4-4] iOS application, *Bloom*

too think it's possible that our grandchildren will look at us in wonder and say, "You mean you used to listen to exactly the same thing over and over again?"

Eno has further developed this generative music with his smartphone application *Bloom*.[fig4-4] As described in a 1995 WIRED magazine interview,[18] it should be "permanently unfinished" work. "What people are going to be selling more of in the future is not pieces of music, but systems by which people can customize listening experiences for themselves. Change some of the parameters and see what you get. So, in that sense, musicians would be offering unfinished pieces of music — pieces of raw material, but highly evolved raw material, that has a strong flavor to it already." Eno's prediction was that he would be able to mix the boxes of multiple artists: for example, multiply the Johannes Brahms and Eno boxes. It's very much a prediction of AI-based composition. Additionally, Eno notes that in the future, he expects new forms of music to emerge at the interface between traditional music, "games" and "demonstrations."

Game AI researcher Yoichiro Miyake points out that the significance of AI's existence in games is to enable, within the scope defined by the game, each player to have a different experience.[19] Take, for example, *No Man's Sky*, released on the PlayStation platform.[fig4-5] [20] In the game players explore the universe, discovering unknown planets, developing various resources, and trying to survive. On the package, the game's sales point is promoted as 18,446,744,073,709,551,616 unique planets and/or ecosystems to play through. The player of the game is both the only one who will experience that exact content, and at the same time, they are also the creator to help materialize it.

Minecraft is the best-selling video game of all time, with 200 million copies sold and 126 million monthly active users as of 2020. It is perhaps the closest thing so far to William Gibson's "consensual hallucination experienced daily by billions of legitimate operators in every nation" cyberspace. In it, players explore and construct elements

[fig4-5] *No Man's Sky*

of a virtually infinite procedurally-generated 3D world. They discover new lands, and others' creations, they craft tools and structures. There are multiple game modes, including ones where players can battle, co-operate, or compete against other players or computer-generated others.

Further into this spectrum of participatory entertainment exist new forms of consumer culture: Reaction videos of listening to music or opening boxed purchases, playing games, or going to websites where such things are going on, and commenting. *Twitch.tv* is a leading live streaming video service for video games in the US, with over 3 million broadcasters monthly and 15 million daily active users, watching 27,000 partner channels of basically anything, from esports to tutorials to bible class to women licking ear-shaped microphones. But all you have to do is participate is to contribute "content." In the world that Eno proposes, producing music, or composing a novel could become like playing a game on *Twitch.tv*, a performer working within a set of constraints, making distinctive choices, which artfully highlight inherent elements of the composition. The more AI is incorporated into the production and performance process, the more vague the boundary between producer and receiver. The "content" is produced by the user's interaction with the AI model.[fig4-6]

Miyake says that the popularity of games such as *Minecraft* lies in the fact that "players do what the creators did in the past." Behind the mechanism where users can freely design furniture and tools, and build huge buildings and parks, the AI is essential for ensuring in-game consistency. Players typically have been protagonists in game narratives, but here, their roles as builders are more strongly reflected. By incorporating AI into the production process, the boundary between creator and audience is blurred. This is what Eno calls the interface between games and demonstrations. The relationship between game broadcasting and AI music generation models points to only a few of the innumerable possibilities which will evolve.

In 1980, futurists Alvin and Heidi Toffler spoke of a post-Industrial

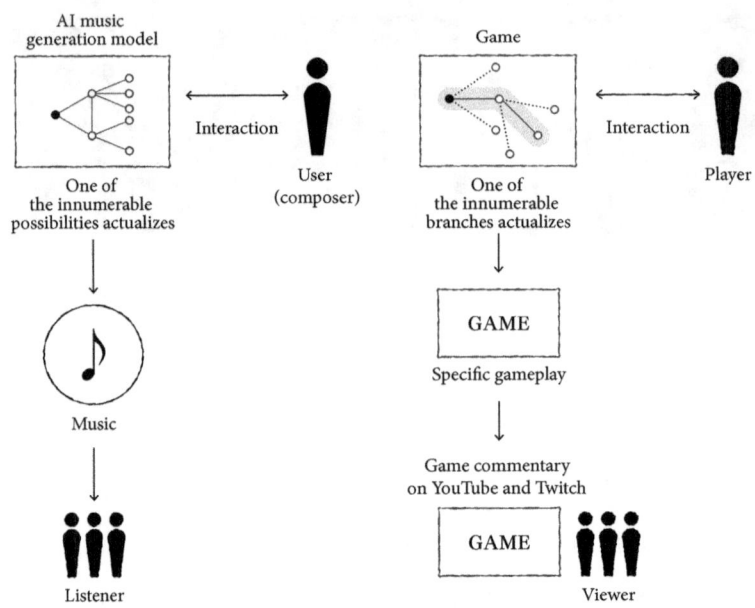

[fig4-6] The relationship between game broadcasting and AI music generation models.

information age of increasingly atomized prosumers.[21] I got a glimpse of a prosumer future when I tried *boomy*,[22] a service by a California-based startup that uses AI to generate songs and publish them on Spotify and Apple Music. "Create original songs in seconds. Release to billions. Submit releases and earn streaming revenue from 40+ services worldwide including Spotify, YouTube, TikTok, and more," the website promises. All you have to do is specify a genre and tempo, and some instrumentation. *boomy* runs an AI simulation and generates options until you decide on something you like. Within five minutes, I was able to submit a song to Spotify. Not only are the album name and artist name randomly assigned by an algorithm, but the album jacket is also generated with AI models. In fact, there are many "artists" who publish using *boomy*. One artist, named Ploosnar, released five 20-track albums on Spotify in 2019 alone.

boomy is the lowest common denominator audio product. The main song elements are sound loops. Originality and taste are effectively irrelevant. What the user is actually doing is just roughly selecting the genre and the tone, so that full AI automation can occur. (Probably designed to skirt the rules of copyright, Spotify, and whatever other music distribution aggregator services they hope to use.) Human will is introduced to create content, which should theoretically connect with humans, in order to generate royalties. I assume that Ploosnar's album tracks will never become hits. My guess would be that, if anything, *boomy* is a model for generating a new variety of down-market muzak, to save on licensing fees for amateur YouTube creators who, again, probably have little qualification to be broadcasting professionals themselves. To whoever uses it, of course, Ploosnar's audio product will always have a special place in their hearts, because that's what music does.

What we see, time and again, is work born not of a traditional work ethic, or by engaging professionals, but rather something culled from a flood of content and the instinct to express, and a set of tools enabling the results into the Internet — itself the pool of content from which AI feeds in the first place, in an overfit self-referential prosumer race to the bottom. But just as platforms like YouTube and Twitch.tv have created new professions that teens aspire to, there is a will to participate which can be harvested. Ten years ago, who knew that you could get paid for opening boxes of products and sharing the experience? What each has in common is that they are worlds where the "play" is participation, like cosplayers or *dojinshi* creators do to participate in anime/manga universes. AI is providing a technological key to bring forth the existence of new cultural aspects and trades which Toffler and Eno anticipated.

In *Noise: The Political Economy of Music*, French polymath Jacques Attali analyzed the history of music by dividing it into four regimes: Sacrificing, Representing, Repeating, and Post-Repeating.[23] In his text *Sacrificial*, he posits that music exists in contrast to the chaotic "noise" of nature. The second Representational regime begins with the introduction of print and copyright, bound to the visual medium of print, but before technologies of automatic reproduction. What was in the first regime the sublimation of nature, in the second regime becomes converted to spectacle, to be re-presented time and again, creating its new opposite, an awed silence, the anticipation of the spectacle. This regime requires increasing complexity and articulation by specialists who, in fact, are exploited and manipulated by capital. The third regime, *Repeating*, represents the entirety of recorded music, from 1900 to the present, including its many ways of distribution. The music itself is no longer a production of complexity but rather of manufactured perfection. In contrast to the dynamism of the specialist offering vivid spectacle, now each artist is bound to repeat some moment of artificial studio perfection, an ever-more-perfect echo of itself, spiraling into a simulacrum of its own existence. The economics of musical consumption shift to a bifurcation between *Exchange-Time*, the time spent earning the money to purchase a recording, and Use-Time, the time spent listening to recordings. One can imagine that Attali's analysis was highly informed by Benjamin's seminal essay, *The Work of Art in the Age of Mechanical Reproduction (1935)*. In it, Benjamin describes how the popularization of reproduction technology would result in the loss of "aura" from art, a loss of uniqueness, of losing the unique moment of appreciating an experience,

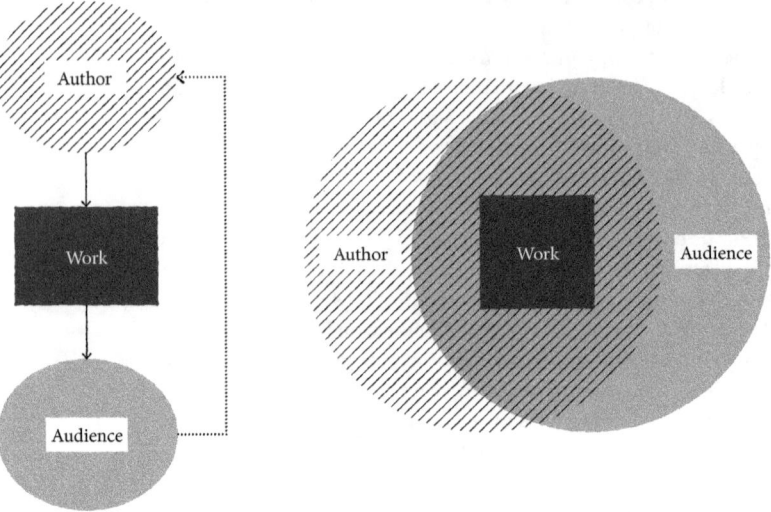

[fig4-7] Author and audience of the AI creation era

and therefore a pivotal moment of socio-technological alienation. He writes: "Great works are no longer considered to be produced by individuals. But rather by groups." The fourth regime, Post-Repeating, is unfortunately largely undeveloped, only described as a "composition system." I imagine it like Eno's "seeds," which never repeat. Compared to preceding systems, it is difficult to explain the composition system in a straightforward manner, but Attali says that it refers to an era in which new musical acts are born; in which performance, listening, and composition are mixed as inseparable. Benjamin writes, "Even the most perfect reproduction of a work of art is lacking in one element: its presence in time and space, its unique existence at the place where it happens to be." This is paradoxically restored by AI, if not at all in the way that Benjamin probably anticipated, because at a press of a button, AI will generate new music - a unique existence in a place and time. In fact, music which has never been played before and may never be again. [fig4-7] And in being a prosumer music, does represent a new cultural heritage, reinforcing memory. It is a ritualized, structured conquering of death, chaos, and destruction of nature.

We are in need of new terms of engagement. These AI-facilitated compositions do not replace traditional compositions any more than the Run DMC replaces Bach. They are another category of thing, just as DJs and sampling are not the songs they represented, yet have expanded the range of musical creative activities. AI breaks with previous concepts of composition, in ways that I, at least, don't have a language to describe. Atali says music is "prophecy." I must say I agree.

Endnotes

1. Kate Crawford, *The Trouble with Bias* (NIPS, 2017)
https://nips.cc/Conferences/2017/Schedule?showEvent=8742
2. Joy Buolamwini, *Gender Shades: Intersectional Accuracy Disparities in Commercial Gender Classification*, Proceedings of Machine Learning Research (2018)
3. Khari Johnson, *ExamSoft's remote bar exam sparks privacy and facial recognition concerns* (09.2020)
https://venturebeat.com/business/examsofts-remote-bar-exam-sparks-privacy-and-facial-recognition-concerns/
4. Sachit Menon, Alexandru Damian, Shijia Hu, Nikhil Ravi, Cynthia Rudin, *PULSE: Self-Supervised Photo Upsampling via Latent Space Exploration of Generative Models* / arXiv:2003.03808v3 [cs.CV] (7.2020)
5. Joni Salminen, Soon-gyo Jung, Shammur Chowdhury, *Analyzing demographic bias in artificially generated facial pictures*, CHI EA'20: Extended Abstracts of the 2020 CHI Conference on Human Factors in Computing Systems (04.2020)
6. Shigeru Hagiwara, *Trends in Foreign Images Appearing in Japanese Television Advertising*, Bulletin of Keio University Media and Communication Research Institute (2004)
7. *Naomi Osaka: Noodle company apologises for 'white-washing'* (BBC News, 01.2019)
https://www.bbc.com/japanese/features-and-analysis-46969435
8. Huawei Launches First Photo Contest Co-Judged by a Phone AI (7.2018)
https://petapixel.com/2018/07/17/huawei-launches-first-photo-contest-co-judged-by-a-phone-ai/.
9. Datasets (ISMIR, 10.2020) https://ismir.net/resources/datasets/
10. *Making hit songs with data-music in the streaming era* (Nihon Keizai Shimbun on-line, 06.2020)
https://www.nikkei.com/article/DGXMZO60010340V00C20A6I00000/
11. OpenAI, *Jukebox* (04.2020) https://openai.com/blog/jukebox/
12. Prafulla Dhariwal, Heewoo Jun, Christine Payne, Jong Wook Kim, Alec Radford, Ilya Sutskever, *Jukebox: A Generative Model for Music* / arXiv:2005.00341v1 [eess. AS] (04.2020)
13. Frank Sinatra was a famously outspoken anti-racist and activist in the Civil Rights Movement.
14. Dani Deahl, Warner Music Signed an Algorithm to a Record Deal – What Happens Next? (The Verge, 03.2019)
https://www.theverge.com/2019/3/27/18283084/warner-music-algorithm-signedambient-music-endel
15. According to 2015 data, 11.6% of all albums released one week were in the sleep and relaxation categories — several times more than genres such as hard rock and Latin pop.
Spotify Data Reveals Boom in Sleep and Relaxation Albums (The Guardian, 09.2015)
http://www.theguardian.com/technology/2015/sep/07/spotify-datasleep-relaxation-albums
16. For example, Endel's Apple Watch app claims to generate personalized music based on heart rate data.
Igor Bonifacic, *Endel's Apple Watch App Generates Soothing Sounds on Your Wrist* (Engadget, 10.2019)
https://www.theverge.com/2019/3/27/18283084/warner-music-algorithm-signed-ambient-music-endel
17. Brian Eno, *A Year with Swollen Appendices* (Faber and Faber, 1996)
18. Kevin Kelly, "I guess the only thing weirder than hearing your own music being broadcast on the radios of strangers is hearing music that you might have written being broadcast!" *Gossip Is Philosophy— Brian Eno Interview* (WIRED, 01.1995)

https://www.wired.com/1995/05/eno-2/
19 *FUTURE by CREATIVITY- What is creativity in the AI era?* (UNIVERSITY of CREATIVITY, 06.2020)
https://uoc.world/articles/details/?id=acahx06xstan detail/?id=mi9wdpg_9
No Man's Sky
https://www.nomanssky.com/
20 No Man's Sky https://www.nomanssky.com/
21 Alvin Toffler, *The Third Wave* (William Morrow, 1980)
22 Boomy, *Make Instant Music with Artificial Intelligence* (https://boomy.com/)
23 Jacques Attali, *Noise: The Political Economy of Music* (English translation, University of Minnesota Press, 1977)

Chapter 5

Tips for working creatively with AI

5.1 Connecting disparate phenomena

Serendipity

t-SNE (t-distributed Stochastic Neighbor Embedding, a nonlinear dimensionality reduction technique) is an algorithm that enables users to visually cluster "high-dimensional" data with similarities together, and separates dissimilarities away from each other in a two or three-dimensional map or model. *Google Arts & Culture* is an online resource featuring content from over 2,000 leading museum and archive sources, and *Google Arts & Culture Experiments*, a showcase for artists and creative coders to present experiments using those archives. The *t-SNE Map*[1] project there has images from the collection organized in three dimensions, almost like a seascape: Horse paintings are clustered in islands, and human portraiture extends out depicting a seashore.[fig5-1] It reminded me of Dawkins' *Biomorph* multiverse, with its scarab beetle hills and weeping willow vales.

The model used here is based on CNN, ANN inspired by the connectivity pattern between neurons that resembles the organization of the animal visual cortex.[fig5-2] Because of the overlapping pattern recognition model it uses, it is relatively suited to GPUs (specialized processors that rapidly batch-manipulate frame buffer memory), enabling the network to learn to optimize autonomously, making it a key technology to sparking the current Deep Learning AI boom.

Allow me to explain how this works: Imagine that you have a piece of paper with an aperture, an open window, with red-colored semi-transparent plastic in it. Using this paper to search through an image stack you find sections that appear black. You identify these as red portions of images. You assign numbers or values to each accordingly. Using a series of other pieces of paper with different colors of

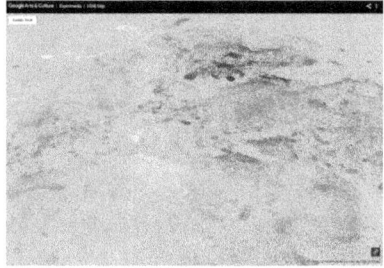

[fig5-1] *t-SNE Map*

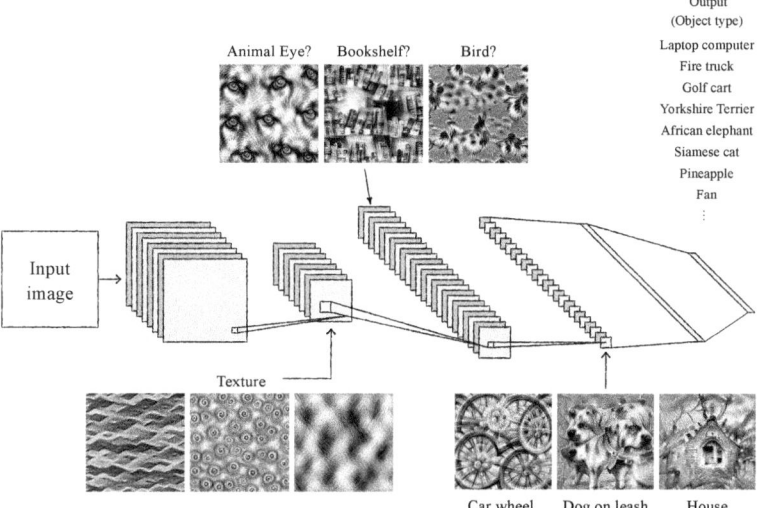

[fig5-2] A schematic diagram of a convolutional neural network (CNN) and an example of an image artificially synthesized so that a specific filter in each layer reacts strongly.

---

transparent plastic — blue, yellow, and other colors or mixtures therein — at some point you would be able to identify each image according to a unique color ratio. Now imagine a second set of papers with shape apertures, to distinguish p's and q's, b's and d's, lowercase l's (L), upper case I's (i), and number 1s. Using this process you would weed out variants in typefaces between Ls and Is, and then other sets to examine variations in the upper and lower left and right sections of each letter. These processes are known as convolutional filtering. Each of these variations would have to be organized according to the resulting values generated. This same general process would be used, on a more complex scale, when filtering for a "car," using stacks of convolutional filters for "tires," "side mirrors," "headlights," etc. Eventually, you might generalize the ability to distinguish between race cars, sports cars, wagons, fire trucks, and golf carts, of each shape and color. CNNs use stacks of many such convolutional filters, and by effectively grouping "trained" (attached appropriate values to) stacks from prolonged exposure to millions of images provided on ImageNet, a visual database of more than than 14 million images designed for use in visual object recognition software research. These stacked convolutional layers might be many thousands of "dimensions," deep, hence the phrase "deep" learning.

The car in this photo is selected based on a combination of CNN filters that have been trained to identify characteristics such as tires and side mirrors, for example. Of course, the AI model has no idea what a side mirror is or why it should be useful. No one specifically modeled the ability to identify specific items in the imagery. Rather, the settings of these filters, and how to combine them, and the relationship between the distribution of reactions to each filter and the object categorizations, develop from numerical correspondences. Densities among such correspondences are called feature vectors, or more simply features, in this case gleaned from the car category. They all have tires in common, but fire trucks are more likely to have a tall, red, square body, whereas golf carts are more likely to feature small tires and a small frame, typically with green grass in the background.[2]

Distinguishing between dogs and other objects is easy for us. I have no problem telling the difference between a Chihuahua and a blueberry muffin, for example, because of the very different relationships I have with each. But most visual ML still struggles with such differences, hence the CAPTCHA tests we've all taken to prove that we're not robots on-line.

The *t-SNE Map* is not a final categorization (of dogs, muffins, golf carts, etc.) but rather part of a series of accumulated calculations. The actual feature vectors are high-dimensional (again, 1,000 or more dimensions), but the nonlinear dimensionality reduction algorithm called *t-SNE* has remapped the high-dimensional feature vector down to, in this case, three dimensions. If two- dimensional is a plane, and three-dimensional is a space, just imagine how complicated a 1,000-dimension vector map would be. Readers with programming experience might easily imagine an array or column of numbers. The art of dimensionality reduction is in how well it retains the relevant variations of the original dataset.

Think of how maps of the Earth are flat, planar depictions of a near-spherical object, yet retaining spatial relationships using Mercator, Azimuthal Equidistant, or other projection systems. In the Mercator projection, for example, the latitude and meridians intersect at right angles, and instead of correctly expressing the angles of all parts of the Earth's surface, the higher the latitude, the more stretched and expressed it becomes. In the same way, the *t-SNE* algorithm converts high-dimensional vector space into a two- or three-dimensional space,

[fig5-3] Gauguin (lower right) and Barrett (upper left) among *ukiyo-e*.

[fig5-4] Van Gogh mixed with old maps. (lower right)

while accurately retaining the spatial relationships from the original high-dimensional dataset.[3]

Mapping the works in *t-SNE Map* this way reveals relationships from the non-human analysis. We notice things like national identity or regional identity, and memes overlap as Chinese prints are placed within the Japanese *ukiyo-e*, as are Western paintings, especially, revealing influences of *ukiyo-e*.[fig5-3] Naturally, Vincent Van Gogh, Paul Gauguin, Edgar Degas, and Henri Matisse can be found amidst Utagawa Hiroshige and Utagawa Kunisada. We expect this because they are Japonists. The English painter and printmaker Charles William Bartlett is nearby. With a little research, I learned that Barrett was actually inspired by *ukiyo-e* as well, and had even visited Japan to study printmaking. We expect these to be here because we understand causality in those relationships, but we didn't tell the AI that we expected them there, and it has no "idea" of whatever causality in their relationships. Of course, there are anomalies as well. Old maps are there with Van Gogh's still-lifes.[fig5-4] Unexpected "similarities" abound. Still, such a bird's-eye view of the features common to many works and their changes over time regardless of the genre, style, or era of art is one of the joys of working with AI. And as the AI improves, we will see further precision in whatever distinctions the AI finds. We may well find new and more obscure meanings and causality, which could make this a surprisingly meaningful resource for art historians. We will learn from AI, and it will learn from us, as technology improves, as does our means of working with it.

In 2019, the author exhibited a system to map the work of designers in the Japan Graphic Designers Association (JAGDA) using the *t-SNE Map* method.[fig5-5] [4] The difference with *t-SNE Map* is that the display could be switched between mapping the features in the

[fig5-5] *JAGDA Map* Installation

lower layers, reflecting properties such as texture, color, simple shape, etc., while the higher layers reflect the object type. We found that being able to compare the different sorting methods was illustrative. Posters advertising the same product series are naturally grouped together, but additionally, designers in master-student relationships, and schools of design, are also mapped in close proximity. It should be emphasized that the similarity here is just a superficial similarity in images as identified within an AI model, and does not carry any considerations of any meaning or concept behind each expression.

Another excellent example from Google Experiments is *X Degrees of Separation*,[5] by Mario Klingemann, an artist introduced in Chapter 1 of this book.[fig5-6] As the title suggests, this work is a play on the *Six Degrees of Separation* hypothesis, the idea that all people on average are six, or fewer, social connections away from each other, and indeed, "Friend Of A Friend" FOAF "too good to be true" spurious Urban Legends. On the website's opening screen, questions such as "What is the connection between a 4,000-year-old clay figure and Van Gogh's *Starry Night*? How do you get from Bruegel's *Tower of Babel* to street art of Rio de Janeiro?" prompt the user to select two works from a database of arts and crafts. Using ML and search algorithms, *X Degrees of Separation* searches the *Google Arts & Culture* database and daisy-chains a set of six works connecting them. Some connections that AI has found are easy to imagine a basis for, such as pairs of works from the same era or region, but connections like the similarities between an 18th-century Tibetan Buddha and a Mesopotamian statue in BC transcend time and space and create new associations, and questions within us. Here Picasso's influence from indigenous African sculpture is evident, but new connections across genres and styles, with or without actual influences or relevances we can yet name become new realizations, new epiphanies. The curiosity, and the serendipity, are entirely within us.

[fig5-6] *X Degrees of Separation* examples

A child's eyes

The image recognition AI used in these two projects has no grasp of whatever historical or geographical context the objects may have, whether African masks, Japanese Noh masks, or a Tahitian girl drawn by Gauguin. It just analyzes the features as an image and connects them according to statistical similarity. The abstract categorizations we use for what we know, or think we know, enable us to function. Our consciousness, our awareness, is a body of internalized classifications, categorizations, and background knowledge that enables higher-level functioning. When I wake up each day, I don't need to process whether or not the sun will rise. I don't need to spend time considering which foot to place where in order to deliver me to my coffee maker. When I see a color, I first process it at low resolution, "it's blue" or "it's yellow" and don't concern myself with whether something is a particular shade of lemon or butterscotch yellow. Linguistic categories translate the high dimensionality we need to process in our minds down to culturally-based symbols, but these symbols and categories can also stand in the way of our seeing the world as it is.

Cognitive scientist Dr. Aya Saito writes of an experiment conducted between chimpanzees who had learned the relationship between colors and writing (the color blue, and the Chinese ideogram for blue) and chimpanzees who had not been so trained, in choosing colors similar to examples shown.[6] When subtle colors such as blue-green were shown, the range of colors recognized differed among chimpanzees, in a sample similar to humans, about whether subtle shades should be classified as blue or green. Interestingly, results showed that chimpanzees who had learned the symbolic expressions demonstrated greater color selection stability, that is, a finer means of categorizing colors, than the chimpanzees who had not. If such a hypothesis is proven true, it could mean enormous implications about the value of language.

There are numerous examples of prominent painters with some

properties of savant syndrome as well as issues with linguistic development; Stephen Wiltshire and Kiyoshi Yamashita, for example. Research suggests that children with savant syndrome capable of drawing highly realistic objective pictures who regain linguistic ability come to draw with more "childish" symbolic subjectivity. Prehistoric cave paintings similarly being quite realistic suggest the lack of symbolic representation, or language, at that time.

AI learns patterns without our culture of symbolic representation. Klingemann's *X Degrees of Separation* works because it is a-symbolic, there is no sense of what are and are not appropriate paths between artworks. In some cases, the connections seem profound, and in others, profane. And therein it makes us question our own systems of categorization. Everyone has memories of looking at clouds in the sky and imagining this one to be a turtle, and that one to be a whale, and so on. AI similarly sees the world fresh and requires us to see the world with children's eyes and see every potential anew, giving us opportunities to revisit our fundamental assumptions, review our data sets, reveal sublimated bias, and question all categorical assumptions.

5.2 Cultivating the uncanny

Interacting with AI

I began DJ-ing as a student. Eventually, I started introducing original material within my sets, and was able to release some of these tracks on labels, and even tour internationally. The frequency of my DJ sets has decreased considerably, but I still can occasionally be found at the turntable in the clubs. DJing is about song selection, the mix, including transitions, scratching, and such, and reading the atmosphere and energy of the room. A DJ's role is to get everyone to loosen up, to both themselves and one another, to inspire them to dance and keep dancing. To build a groove you usually want to stay in a kind of tonal envelope, but a great DJ also knows how to spice things up from time to time to keep it fresh. But anybody who's performed any creative act over 20 years knows that you can sometimes feel like you're in a rut.

A back-to-back DJ set, or B2B set, is when two DJs play a kind of dialogue set, ricocheting back and forth off one another, each highlighting their own styles and personalities, creating new tensions, contrasting and complimenting each other. The way they pass-off to one another, like jazz players, or any other improvisational art, will be about trying to elevate each other's "game." I decided to create an AI DJ to help me analyze the essence of what I was doing, or trying to do, and use AI to move me out of my rut, and in 2015 this resulted in the *AI DJ Project*.[fig5-7] [7] People tend to misunderstand it. The point was never to automate my flow or replace myself with an AI version of myself. Rather, I just wanted a fresh perspective on who and what I was as a DJ. In order to do that, and "disrupt" my own style, I developed an AI DJ to do B2B sets with.[fig5-8] [8]

In other words, it was a project that I started with the idea that I could reproduce that special tension through interaction with AI. The art of the DJ is expressed through song selection, mixing them and scratching to create something unexpected, and greater than the sum of their parts, all while meaningfully engaging the atmosphere and energy of the room.[9] The first thing for the AI to learn was the song selection. Thinking about the lessons of art works like *t-SNE Map* or *X Degrees of*

[fig5-7]
AI DJ Project,
2017
Shibuya WWW

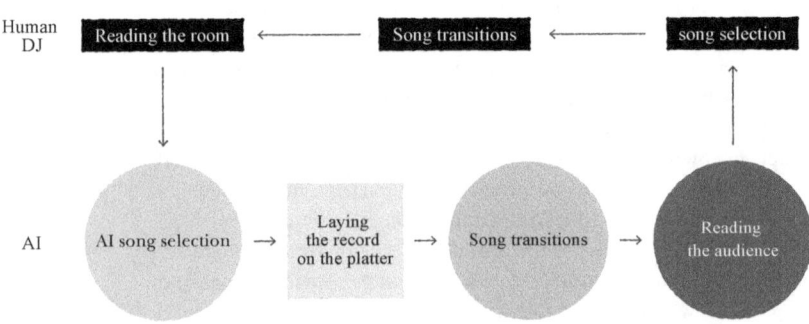

[fig5-8] The AI DJ project process. A person puts the records selected by AI on the turntable.

144

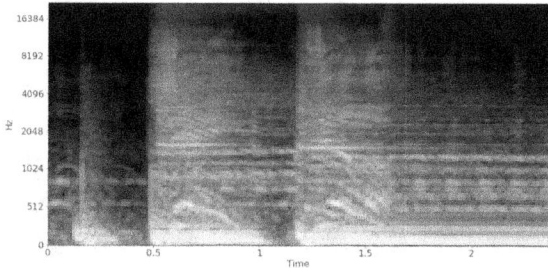
[fig5-9] A spectrogram

Separation, I realized that mapping my music would be one solution. Sound is treated as image data, expressed as a spectrogram, the length of time on the horizontal axis and audio frequency on the vertical axis.[fig5-9] After collecting a sufficient volume of music I built a *CNN* model which recognized song genres, instrumentation, etc. from each spectrogram. With *AI DJ*, I was able to work with the differences between the output of multiple models, including those trained by music genre and instrumentation, and combining and mapping those, compared with *t-SNE Map*, which essentially maps single object features. It was interesting to see how and what the AI learned about how musical genre distinctions and instrumentation impacted its output, including its "sense" of rhythmic composition, groove, tempo, timbre, and such.

Part of the learning data process was collecting playlists from famous DJs, a historical element. I was able to use the concept of cooperative filters to teach the AI how to estimate which songs play well together, like the shopping prompt "People who buy that product also buy this product" kind of technology.[fig5-10] The song selections created in this way didn't have issues, but they weren't interesting either. It was a real "meh" moment because averaging among the safest options can only produce mediocrity. Playing it safe is not the path out of a creative rut. The updated system no longer reflects the famous DJ song selection knowledge base and selects songs based purely on the similarity of musical elements. But it was a good lesson. Each time I perform, I'm debugging the latest update.

The resulting musical "map" had clusters reminiscent of the *ukiyo-e* island or portrait coast in *t-SNE Map*. Drum'n'bass and dubstep were continents with tectonic bass, and Chicago House appeared as its own peninsula. On closer inspection, I discovered a cluster of organ-based songs on one part of the Chicago house promontory. It can be hard to put into words the impressions and moods one encounters when listening to a song, as compared to a visible painting, for example, but an AI model can hypothetically quantify musical characteristics

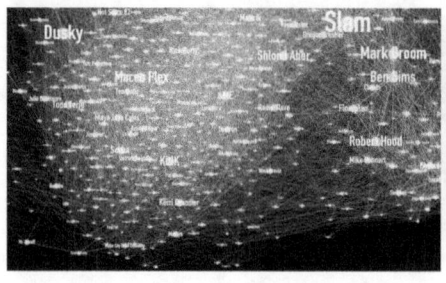 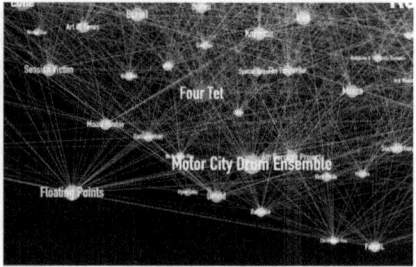

[fig5-10] Visualizations of famous DJs' playlists.

and organize them for you. And once you have your modeling system in place, you can explore the terrain, and see where a given song is, and where other DJs travel in your musical map.[10] Of course, you, as a DJ, can then select new mood topographies. As with Klingemann's *X Degrees of Separation*, I tried interpolating songs across a virtual line connecting the spectrogram images, extrapolating trajectories based on song pairs that the AI, and human me played in our B2B battles. In AI B2B, the "flow" and "groove" are, at least partially, functions of inertia.[fig5-11] [11]

I came of age in an era when people still used vinyl, but nowadays more and more people are DJ-ing using software. In addition to the health benefits of not always having to carry huge and heavy boxes of records, DJ software handles tempo and beat matching[12] at the touch of a button. In the *AI DJ project*, I wanted to use turntables and vinyl records which need to have technical issues like tempo and beat matching, and failures to mix, to better visualize the AI DJ's behavior, and make it less "black box." To that end, I worked with the YCAM Interlab, the research and development team of YCAM (Yamaguchi Center for Arts and Media, a media art center in southwest central Japan) to create a computer-controlled turntable.

During a rehearsal one day, I played a techno classic from around 2000. In response, the AI DJ picked a contemporary track, somewhere between what I might call ambient and free jazz. I couldn't imagine the two working, but it was only a rehearsal, so I played it. A completely addictive fresh mix was born.[13] I vividly remember getting goosebumps from the shock of this discovery. I still get goosebumps remembering it as I write this today. I really felt thankful for my AI DJ's input that day. It taught me that I am sometimes a prisoner of my own habits, and limitations in how I process genre and era.

Other DJs have tried out AI DJ, and the response has been good for song selection continuity, but they generally point out the lack of a flow or direction. One thing that experience as a DJ makes you aware

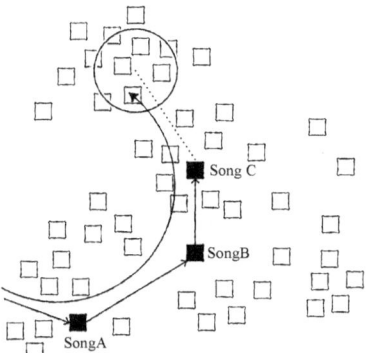

[fig5-11] AI DJ song selection mechanism (conceptual diagram)

of is different kinds of "flow." I agree that the current selection can feel ad hoc. My current AI DJ system only considers the last few songs. But it's worth repeating that my intention was never to automate DJing or create some kind of perfect DJ robot. Whether we like it or not, software will continue to advance, automating elements of many quantifiable tasks, be it DJing or whatever. So I think that it's worth taking up the challenge and including idiosyncratic analog equipment (a turntable) in my system, to ask the question, "What is the essence of DJing in a world that is increasingly software dominant?" My goal is to gain a deeper understanding of the essence of DJing (or an examination of my own DJing) through externalizing it in building an AI DJ, much like Cohen pursued his interest in exploring his painting process and the essence of art, by building a robot which objectified his own subjective approach.

After a European tour in 2017 and 2018 (France, Slovenia, and Romania), I was invited to present the AI DJ as the opening act of Google's largest annual developer conference, Google I / O, in 2019. This is me, co-starring with AI DJ in front of more than 15,000 people, just before Google CEO Pichai Sundararajan's keynote.[fig5-12]

License to ill

Less successful were my attempts at using AI to "read the room." As part of my AI DJ set-up, I installed a camera to identify human skeletal structure so that I could include dance participation in my dataset of songs and mixes.[fig5-13] The optimal state is a dance floor full of vigorously moving bodies throughout the course of a DJ set. This should inform an AI DJ's travels through the musical map. Relatively less bodily engagement, including reduced activity and fewer bodies on the dance floor, both might indicate a specific song in the landscape, or it might indicate a fatigue about that area of the musical map, like an environmental issue, where the natural resources of that area have been depleted. In such situations, the AI should have mechanisms for abrupt [fig5-12] *AI DJ Project*, Google I/O 2019 Keynote Pre-show

[fig5-13] *AI DJ Project*, YCAM (December 2017)

leaps into other parts of the terrain.

I designed this part of the system on old-school, rule-based AI. First I used DL to quantify body movements, but the mechanisms for jumps across the landscape were based on my own discretion. I debuted this system at YCAM in 2017. Drops in dancer engagement caused the AI to jump to distant areas on the musical landscape, and the idea was to introduce elements to attract more dancers, but the AI would double-down on the intensity of those jumps, and expel those dancers with the next track, to another unrelated aesthetic, and so on. A balance between predictability and the unexpected is essential to attracting crowds to the dance floor, but this functioned more like a centrifuge, repelling people away. But it was a good edge-case lesson in the art of

[fig5-14] AKAI MPC3000 sampler used by Dilla.

DJing, and how delicate the art of transitions can be.

In AI, we typically look for edge cases to identify "boundaries," because if we can locate overlaps where the technology is applicable, then we can be sure of coverage. But in the creative arts, consistent coverage may not be what we're after. Edge models are opportunities for creative leaps. Edge models are more like style and humor, which are often about leaps, "misalignments," "mismatches," and "gaps." The Monty Python line, "You must cut down the mightiest tree in the forest with…a herring!" works because of the absurdity is informed by the average Brit's relationship with herrings, "kippers." In data, there is the center, and then edge models, like humor, which introduces a specific sense of incongruity or tension, and then defuses, clarifies, or upends that tension with a secondary proposition or idea. Metaphors, similes, allusions, twists, implied and explicit are all factors in taking things out of context, playing between categories of knowledge.

To me, the definitive genius of "misalignments," "mismatches," and "gaps," of freedom from edge cases and "boundaries," was Soulquarian J Dilla (Jay Dee),[14] arguably one of the greatest producers hip-hop ever produced. His one-of-a-kind AKAI MPC series sampler alchemy radiates throughout the legacies of A Tribe Called Quest, D'Angelo, Erykah Badu, and so many other masterpieces.[fig5-14] Rhythm in electronic music is typically driven by drum machines and samplers. We tap small drum-like pad interfaces on the machine, assigned with percussive sounds, whether they be kicks and hi-hats or whipping chains against a concrete floor, into memory. Most people input these using quantization, and auto-correct, to force what they've played in sync with the internal metronome clock in the machine. But never J Dilla.[15] In songs like Pharcyde's *Bullshit*, he drags a kick drum, inconsistent across verses, slightly behind the beat, against all rules, creating a deep funk epiphany. According to ?uestlove, it was "the most life-changing moment I ever had… It sounded like the kick drum was played by a drunk 3-year-old ."[16] The unconventional ways he worked with MPC samplers changed

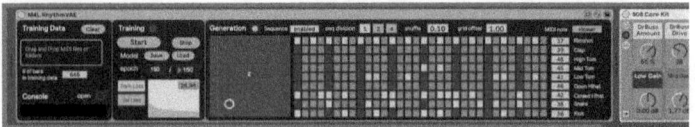

[fig5-15] M4L.RhythmVAE rhythm generation plug-in

hip-hop, opening up new rhythm sensibilities which continue to impact people, both those working in machine-generated rhythms and those working in non-machinic alike. Here again, we see the influence of machine-generated expressions adding to the palette of human expression.

I developed the M4L.RhythmVAE rhythm generation software plug-in so that even artists unfamiliar with AI can generate new rhythms in common music production software by just dragging and dropping musical data.[fig5-15] [17] It detects the attack of each beat, and looks to model the "misalignments," "mismatches," and "gaps," of interest. It's because it is unmatched in its accuracy that it has the liberty to shift accurately.

Every time dancers' interest seemed to lag, Martindale's "arousal potential" is engaged and songs that betray expectations in interesting ways draw them back onto the dance floor. AI is a new suite of technologies cultivating the uncanny valley, paying homage to our inheritance of flow and groove, mixing things up in new ways to generate a new literacy of interesting gaps and misalignments.

[fig5-16] *Israel* & イスラエル

5.3 Embracing heterogeneity

Alien intelligence(s)

Israel Galván, beloved for his complicated rapid-fire dancing, dramaturgy, and choreographic flair, is an *enfant terrible*, a revolutionary, in the flamenco avantgarde. At the end of 2017, I was invited to create a collaboration with Israel at YCAM.[fig5-16] [18] "Flamenco? Why me?" I asked. "Because flamenco is music" was the reply. Flamenco is a highly complex performance art form built from three fundamental elements — *cante*, singing; *toque*, guitar; and *baile*, dance — though it is also known, under avant-garde artists like Israel who voraciously explore many other forms of expression as well. Flamenco is rooted in traditions from Andalucia, southernmost Spain, or perhaps the gypsies there, who were originally called *gitanos* or *flamencos* (a corruption of the Arabic *felag mangu*, or "fugitive peasants"). The music of flamenco is built around the *compás* metronomic system, primarily in a 12-beat measure structure. To Israel, and the *baile*, the *sapateado* (rhythmic foot motions, like tap dance) is the pulse of flamenco, the *palma* (hand claps) is its counter-rhythms. The melody of body and hand arises through

[fig5-17] *Arena*, MITO Settembre Musica, *6.IX Israel Galván #1*

them. My job, therefore, needed to be rooted in Israel's *sapateado*.

Raised in a family of flamenco dance, Israel's career has been one of reclaiming flamenco, refuting the nationalist kitsch reputation some felt it had gained under Franco, and elevating both its fundamentals, and its capabilities, as a form of high-modern expression. Debuting in his teens, Israel had already won "just about every top flamenco prize possible" by his 20s. He created his own flamenco company in his 30s, and has now gone solo, remaining committed to expanding Flamenco's vocabulary, and developing large-scale pieces such as his own version of Kafka's novelette Metamorphosis; Arena, a choreography set in a bullfighting ring; and Solo, a work forgoing all music except the rhythms created by his own body.[fig5-17] Yet however complex the mise en scene, each saw Israel dancing with inanimate objects, where the echo call-and-response to his dancing would have been predictable.

When YCAM first approached him, it wasn't originally with the idea of a collaboration with me, or with AI. But I happened to be working there with Mitsuto Ando on my *AI DJ project* at that time, and it seemed, like Harold Cohen's *Aaron*, an excellent opportunity to externalize and quantify my own creative process. Israel was intrigued, saying "I want to dance with my alter ego… a partner like Sancho Panza for Don Quijote." He had the same sense of issue as me. But the issues of mapping my DJing, and exploring real-time *sapateado* were quite different. Firstly, there was no existing body of data to start the training. No one had ever recorded the *sapateado*, or *compás* for training AI models before. We needed to create flamenco dancing shoes with sensors embedded and create our own training dataset.

I worked with engineers from the YCAM Interlab to make shoes equipped with piezo sensors, gyro sensors, and pressure sensors to triangulate Israeli's *sapateado*, whether being generated from the heel, toe, or pad of the foot.[fig5-18] However hard you imagined it this might be to do, believe me, it was much much harder than that. We spent weeks building the first pair. Israel broke them in seconds. We needed them to

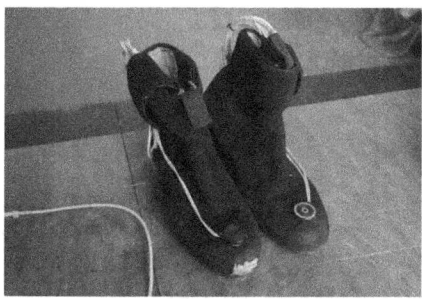
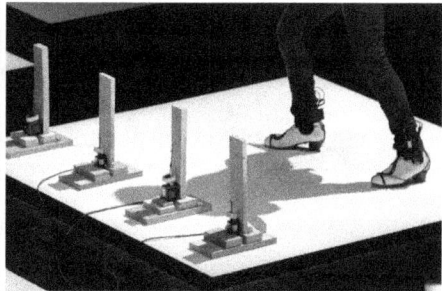

[fig5-18] Data-capture boots for Galvan's *sapateado*.

[fig5-19] Solenoid mechanism for producing the AI-generated "Sancho Panza" counter-point rhythms.

---

last through an entire dance program, and function wirelessly, sending data to our computers at a temporal resolution (sampling frequency) greater than 100 samples per second. I then needed to convince Israel, who is not a fan of repetition, to repeat exactly the same *compás* over and over again so that I could verify my data.

The engineering of Israeli's shoes finally stabilized, allowing us to record his *sapateado* and generate training data from it. It also allowed us to use data from his shoes, in real-time performance, as an input device to generate a predictive AI *sapateado*, a "Sancho Panza" counter-point to his "Quijote." I tried numerous possibilities for output. I tried an LSTM like Douglas Eck had. After a time, I settled on dividing the data per *compás*, within a fine grid of triangulation data from the shoes, for left and right foot each, including their strength and deviations from each previous *compás*.[19] In order to avoid anthropomorphization, we used analog electromechanical solenoids, created by Kanta Horio, to strike the wooden stage floor.[fig5-19] Faithful Sancho would exist as a kind of echo. As I collected data, and trained the *sapateado* generation models, trying different ways to quantify and verify the results, I would check with Israel, whose responses would typically be something like "It's too flamenco" or "I don't need a downgraded version of myself." And that is the essence of the problem. It's not for me, as someone collaborating using AI, to create a lesser mimicry of, or simplify, his work. I needed to learn Israel's flamenco, in some definition of its true essence, well enough to be able to deviate in a way that elevated his art. I studied, and captured data on complex flamenco rhythms such as *bulerías* and *seguiriyas*, as well as his freestyle improvisations, and figured out how to teach the AI how to randomly sample this inheritance into generative models as probability distributions. There were issues about where to place on the grid to emphasize or nullify deviations within the learning model. There is an art to taking something delicate and profound, and then introducing random distortion, just enough to inspire.

To understand this random sampling, imagine that Israel is a gambler at a roulette wheel which I, the croupier, have modified, drilling holes of varying sizes into the dish. Israel dances a set of movements, placing his bet, and I set the roulette wheel in motion, balls spinning. Probability says that the greater odds are for larger holes to have more balls falling through them. The first beat of the *compás* is more or less guaranteed to be an opening beat, so that was given the largest hole. The distribution of hole sizes was made across a proportional representation of the knowledge we gained from studying his dancing. That's how the rhythm generation model worked. The larger and more regularly you make large holes, and the smaller you make the smaller holes, the less surprising the rhythms become. All holes being the same size would create complete randomness, devoid of any language. The trick is to distribute the variations of holes to create unexpected results, within the parameters of Israel's art. The parameter that controls this randomness is called temperature and is often used when utilizing generative models. In this performance, we controlled the 'expressiveness' of the *sapateado* by increasing or decreasing the temperature value from scene to scene.

After months of trial and error, *Israel & イスラエル* (*Israel & Israel*. We used the Japanese syllabary to represent the sound of his name, as a grapheme representing the cross-cultural collaboration, and to highlight the otherness of him working with an AI model trained on himself) premiered on February 2, 2019. After the premiere, Israel called me over, his face beaming, and said, "It was like dancing with something unknown. Not a human in the first place, certainly not a flamenco dancer. I felt like there were aliens with me on stage. It was very inspiring." "For a moment, while I was dancing, I forgot I was alone." This was the best possible compliment for me, and everyone else on the team, as our intention was to stimulate Israel's creativity, by employing a heterogeneity unique to AI. Originally looking to break the frame of his own dance by engaging an unknown thing, and aided by the balance between predictability and unpredictability unique to AI, his dancer's instincts were stimulated. I embraced this comment. Yes, AI is also Alien Intelligence,[20] not bound by human common sense or patterning. Israel didn't want to dance with the AI system until just before the performance (which worried the production team in every way imaginable). But Israel's desire was to be genuinely "surprised," and at the same time showed his supreme confidence that he could respond to whatever the AI produced.

Rewind, to the summer of 2018, a half-year before the premiere. I had flown to Israel's hometown of Seville with the YCAM Interlab staff to deliver the new data collection shoes, set up the computer environment in his studio, and discuss details of the performance. During my off-hours, I would wander the streets of Seville, taking in shows at a *tablao*, a storied flamenco venue, to gain a deeper understanding of the culture. I fell in love with the spontaneous arising in the songs and dances at the taverna throughout the city. On this occasion, in the middle of the room, an elderly woman, in a fine voice, was finishing

[fig5-20] A scene from a *tablao*, in Seville, Spain.

a rousing song.[fig5-20] A young maiden quietly stepped forward and began to dance. The society surrounding her sang, danced, and clapped, in rhythm, much like the breath of life. This was the blessing of their cultural inheritance. A world of implicit grace. The hurdles we faced, unknowingly, were all to introduce a whole new set of values into this world, already so much part of their soil and blood. At that moment, and amidst that community, I truly did feel the oriental, the outsider. I could see, at once, why Israel did not want to only stay in this circle of flamenco culture, and what a beautiful thing Israel Galván was trying to do, in expanding flamenco's potential through dancing with AI.

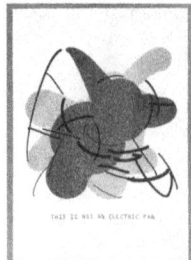

[fig5-21] *Perception Engines*

5.4 Value misconversion

Misunderstanding

Generative Art is a conceptual art form in which the work is aided by an autonomous agent, for example, computers, physics, or chance.[21] Creative coding is much more specifically computer related, though both have often been used to describe art made with the aid of information technology. *Perception Engines*, is an excellent example of both generative art and creative coding, by New Zealand artist and Victoria University of Wellington School of Design lecturer Tom White. [fig5-21] [22] White first decides on a subject, for example, an electric fan. He initiates his system, which outputs a series of shapes, lines, and colors. White then applies a general recognition model to this series and measures their ability to be recognized as the specified object, an electric fan. At first, it is, of course, almost zero. Then White has the program add random pictorial elements, circles and lines, and colors, and selects or rejects each of these and filters again and again, in a way that they are recognized more as an electric fan. This must create millions of iterations. Imagine doing a Google image search for "electric fans," which is something like what the image recognition model dataset has to start from. I just did, and found everything from stand-alone room fans to huge restaurants ventilation systems to CPU cooling systems. How many paintings are there in the fan-themed abstract genre? Rather, in this case, we have only image recognition. Formulating a conception of fan-ness from a keyword search in a database, rather than from the experience of having used or been taught about fans, seems impossible. The image recognition model then needs to decipher, based on purely visual criteria, commonalities and differences, to derive its algorithms.

Eventually, the ML is able to search its way toward images that fit within the ML's recognition parameters for the specified object. Upon completion White proofs the results by testing if they are identifiable to the same ANN that initiated them, as well as to major AI image recognition systems such as those developed by Google and Amazon. He continues to refine the work by making prints in varying color palettes and angles, including adding elements like lens distortion. All of this is to verify it as "art for AI, by AI. By giving the algorithms a voice to speak in, we are better able to see the world through the eyes of a machine." In liberating the aesthetics of the artwork from being good or bad or novel among paintings, we have expressions that are truly of an AI-native genre. Philosophers Gilles Deleuze and Felix Guattari describe art as an abstract machine resistant to representation. Like Babbage and Loveless's *Analytical Engine*, White's *Perceptual Engine* is a conceptual art machine generating post-representation. Perhaps Lovelace already was predicting this in the early 19C. I wish we could hear her comments about this alternate intelligence, with "no pretensions to originate anything."

What can we, non-AI humans, say about the archetypes produced? It's not Rene Magritte's *The Treachery of Images (This is Not a Pipe)*. White's original title was to be *The Treachery of ImageNet* — the name of the image dataset — in homage to Magritte. If you asked a child to paint a fan, it would be rooted in general experience. If you asked a savant, it would likely be one very specific fan. This is neither, nor the Obvious group's random pre-modern bourgeoisie portrait averaging. It's abstract, but not symbolic. Unlike the zero-sum world of Go, the rules are not clear in artistic expression, and it is therefore impossible for AI to assign a symbolic value to it. No matter how realistic the pipe might have been drawn by Magritte, it was only ever a pattern of oil and pigment on canvas, made art by an artist capable of triggering a sense of pipe-ness within our symbolic functionality, and making us aware of that relationship. Despite White's "for AI, by AI" protestations, the *Perception Engine*, i.e., the production system framework itself, is by Tom White. It was White who chose the algorithm and set the learning framework. But in doing so, he made great art, because White created a system where AI needed to make explicit what it considers fan-ness. And makes us aware that AI's fan-ness is not our fan-ness, and is not even rooted in the same set of references. And that is original, and it expands the overall framework of visual learning. It's not art meant to be representing human experience, but it is a brilliant case of creativity via

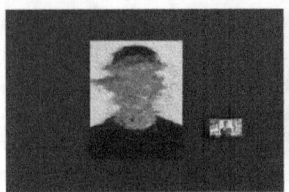
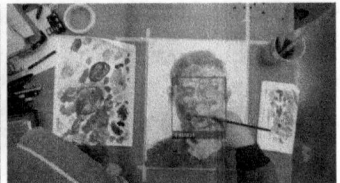

[fig5-23] *Nonfacial Portrait*

[fig5-22] Sen no Rikyū, *Bamboo Flowerpot*

value mis-conversion.

Misunderstanding AI

To a Japanese, this AI misunderstanding communicates as a case of *mitate*, or "likening" things to one another, to provide a kind of channel to other associations. There is some overlap with the idea of the metaphor, but the function and effect are different and worth distinguishing. The typical example of *mitate* is the rock garden, where raked sand can create allusions to sea waves or waterfalls, surrounded by hedges subtly sculpted to "borrow" distant mountain-scapes or suggest poetic references. In contemporary design, Yasuhiro Suzuki created a huge zipper fastener to ride on waterways, opening the lake to reflections of the sky and waves in its wake. Philosopher, priest, and Japanese *Way of Tea* art form innovator Sen no Rikyū was a symbolic category re-mix master of the wry *mitate* allusion, pun, or incongruity. In one famous example, he used vernacular fish baskets to hold his flower arrangements in high tea before the nation's most powerful lords.[23]
[fig5-22] *Mitate* works like humor, in that it introduces a fresh sense of incongruity or tension, but with *mitate*, each individual provides their own reading of how to resolve the tension. *Mitate* is a mechanism of value conversion. Like montage in film, new value can be created, and new associations and points of reflection are cultivated. Just like the most influential work of modern art can be a repurposed urinal *Fountain*, and the most valued Japanese tea implements are those with patina, cracked and re-paired, their humble repairs emphasized, a new value is created not in a single-use discarding of AI mis-apprehensions, but rather when they can be made anew and reflected on, as fodder for new perspectives and another, albeit non-human, intelligence.

The prehistoric parietal cave art in the Altamira Caves was extruded from patterns in existing cracks in the cave walls, showing that primitive humans must have been inspired to embellish upon them.[24]

[fig5-24] An image generated by *DeepDream*.

A toddler given a piece of paper with facial contours will draw eyes and a nose. An infant will trace the outline and then wrinkle it or strike or wrinkle the paper. It's not a blank canvas to them yet. Nor is it for a chimpanzee. Something about the development of our intelligence is an evolved pattern recognition to imagine what is not there.

A personal favorite artwork of mine, which uses ML computer algorithms developed to improve automatically through "experience," is *Nonfacial Portrait*[25] by Korean artist group Shinseungback Kimyonghun. [fig5-23] As the title suggests, the work deals with portraiture. A human painter begins drawing a portrait. A camera captures the developing image and feeds this data to the facial recognition ML algorithms, and the ML indicates each time it starts to be able to recognize the resulting drawing as a face. A game of cat-and-mouse ensues, with the painter developing the portrait, but in ways which avoid recognition by the ML as a portrait. Here we see an externalization of cognitive and evaluation criteria — essential for any artwork production process — in concert with the ML facial recognition algorithms, in a race to depict the literal frontiers of portraiture. *Nonfacial Portrait* is both an example of exploratory creativity using ML to invert traditional portraiture, and at the same time an exploration of transformational creativity to clarify portraiture's limits.

Deep Dream[26] is a well-known experiment in DL, using image recognition models to identify objects and then modify the images so as to further emphasize them in terms of machine-recognizable features, resulting in fractal psychedelic nightmares.[fig5-24] Dogs and clouds shaped like dogs and everything else is drawn into a recognition loop, resulting in entire landscapes of AI dog-ness hallucination, because dogs dominate nearly 100 out of the 1,000 categories in ImageNet, the dataset used to train the image recognition models. Maybe *Deep Dream* was the chimpanzee, and White's *Perception Engine* was the child. Over time we will learn how AI logic is different from humans, and if there are developmental factors that will bring us closer.

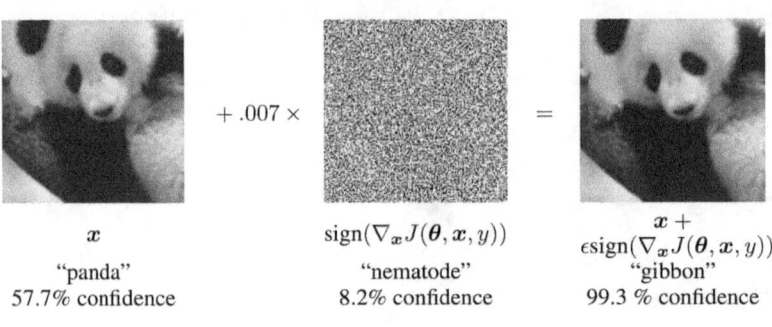

[fig5-24] Examples of Adversarial Examples that misidentify pandas as gibbons.

It is common hacker practice to create image recognition camouflage, adding noise invisible to the human eye into images to create specific forms of mis-recognition. Watermarks help manage paper trails in a paperless world. But seemingly harmless graffiti can be made to trick autonomous vehicle AI, convincing it that a stop sign is an 80-mph speed limit. Such Adversarial Examples pose serious threats in an AI world, and a great deal of research is underway to counter their security threats.[fig5-25] [27]

Just as COVID has tested the social contract in many societies, the rise in "smart city" surveillance technology, DL AI facial recognition technology is getting a lot of sample data, pushing forward questions of the balance of individual privacy and social order. When I get in a cab in Tokyo, the camera instantly grasps data about me, and immediately begins making assumptions about race and gender and such, on the premise of feeding me better-targeted advertising. Philip K. Dick's signature paranoia, so vividly presented in Steven Spielberg's 2002 film *The Minority Report*, an extrapolation of Dick's short story about police working with "precogs" to stop crime before it exists, comes to mind. (Or the "predictive policing" of contemporary urban life.)

My students and I developed camouflage uniforms for the 21st century using such Adversarial Examples[fig5-26], like an homage to Shinseungback Kimyonghun's *Nonfacial Portrait*.[28] In the absence of sufficient public debate about a totalitarian AI surveillance society and runaway capitalism, we created camouflage uniforms to reduce the rate of being identified as a "human." Like Obi-Wan Kenobi, we wanted to tell AI "these are not the humans you're looking for" and so named it *UN-LABELED*.[29] Technically, it's the exact opposite of *Deep Dream*. Whereas *Deep Dream* dreamt of puppy dogs, our image recognition model makes the AI loop away from being able to recognize us as "human." Of course, it's limited to the surface areas covered in our camouflaged clothing. To develop it, we created 3D scans of bodies and ran simulations in various environments to be able to dissociate the bodies inside as coherent

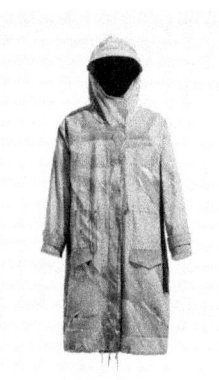 

[fig5-25] *UNLABELED – Camouflage Against the Machines*

while wearing them. Camouflage is always in fashion, so I hope that this provides a strategy while we begin to have the discussions necessary for such highly surveilled urban lifestyles.

5.5 Tips for creatively interacting with AI

How to interact with AI

And so our time together draws to a close. In closing, here are some humble suggestions for expanding creativity by interacting with computational rule-based systems, or AI. As I wrote in the Introduction, everything started for me with a desire to make creative, original music, despite the fact that I couldn't play or read.

1. Let AI "impersonate."

Do what you do well. Use AI as a mirror. Like Harold Cohen's *AARON*, start with trying to clarify the essence of what you do by letting it imitate you. But don't try to create a perfect mirror image. It's art. You're looking to emphasize, or distort. There are sweet spots, certain aspects, and characteristics you will want it to impersonate. Refine. Remember Hatsune Miku and the *TR-808*. Imperfections and limitations, strange caricatures give rise to new ideas and unique new ways of working.

2. Value AI's "mistakes and unpredictability."

Let people's conventions, methods, formulas, and common sense be the "correct answers," and spur AI to be the one that makes interesting "mistakes." But being just random is literally pointless. Think of Martindale's evolution of art and the Wundt curve, anything that is too out of the ordinary will be rejected. Stay within inspiring feedback loops. Giants like Pollock and Cage and Burroughs used random and stochastic processes to break out of and redefine their respective fields. I think that's something for human talent. In my experience, AI is more productive in generating "moderate" deviations, half a step outside the known area, where the degree of deviation is relatively easy to control. Even *Dilbert* creator Scott Adams says: "Creativity means allowing yourself to make mistakes, and art means choosing which mistakes to make." In other words, let's use AI to spark your creativity, and then choose which ones to keep.

3. Become an AI "gardener."

In my book, I've tried to introduce AI systems and work which I found inspirational. But imagine if you were to design your own system and apply it to your own creative practice. It's an architectural task, building the concept for a system, and planning how to structure the system. AI models are, in fact, called "architecture" and the term "AI architect" is beginning to become common, and for "building" AI systems. Architects and designers of course have structural issues. This is probably true for forms like autonomous vehicles or stock trading, in which case predictability is everything.

I would make a distinction between AI architects and AI gardeners. In my case, I find interesting varieties to plant and prune, and I anticipate that unpredictable things will happen.[30] Naturally, gardeners are caring for living things, and in many cases, they are meaning to produce for the good of others. They are stewards of gardens with historical or aesthetic merit, or those which produce useful things. When creating an AI system, you do select an architecture that suits your purpose and feed it learning data. You will grow a lot of weeds, and some beautiful flowers will come from unexpected places. Like horticulture, you need to respect the others' process, and not try to control everything. Try different levels of control, and try to remain conscientious of the power of delegating, and rethinking your expectations. I think that you have to have an attitude of being ready to accept whatever is born and be prepared to love it. Then, like Karl Sims' *Galapagos*, it only takes relatively simple rules for evolution to occur. The important thing is not to try to control everything.

Or maybe let's say that the places you need total control over should remain the human elements. Creating within controlled parameters is more efficient, and I will design sections in advance, but that can also be me being afraid to push myself. If the point is to make creative music that no one has ever heard before then I need to step outside of what I can prepare under controlled parameters. For me, AI is a tool for gathering interesting possibilities from "outside" of that safe area that I hadn't anticipated or knew existed.[31]

4. "Misuse" AI.

Tom White used image recognition AI to draw abstract paintings. That's exactly backwards. Robin Sloan complicated his novel-writing

[fig6-1] A horseless carriage under the Red Flag Act.

process and harvested what he found interesting from a sentence generation model. They both expected that by using AI in ways other than those originally envisioned, they would be able to direct their creations beyond their comfort zones or even places they recognized. And they were right. We are used to the idea of AI existing for optimization, but in our case, we need to imagine that it is for producing diversification. *Teachable Machine* by Google allows you to easily create image recognition models without any knowledge of ML just using your webcam. The ability to export trained models and incorporate them into your own software has led to a variety of great creative misuses. Runway ML, operated by the New York startup Runway, provides one such example. Using their software, users can try out the latest AI models and learn GAN manipulation based on their own images. This kind of AI democratization is really heathy. By creating an environment where anyone can freely misuse AI tools, a greater range of participants can participate, and hopefully open completely unimagined new horizons.

Me, I'm headed back to my laboratory. If AI represents the *Library of Babel* of all known expressions and ideas, then we've still just stepped into the foyer. The library, as a metaphor for the possible, is filled with endless rooms which spread out before us, which nobody's even thought to set foot in yet. Some have been locked closed for no good reason at all. Starting those adventures will never be easier than right now. If, through the efforts of writing this book, even one new traveling companion might emerge, or if eventually, even some slight contribution to a richer expansion of humanity's *Library of Babel* is a result, then, "My solitude is gladdened by this elegant hope."

Postscript: AI surfing

Maybe we should just retire the phrase "artificial" intelligence, and switch to "alternative" intelligence instead. Automobiles were briefly called "horseless carriages," just as mobile phones were called "wireless,"

[fig6-2] *Brian Eno's The Ship — A Generative Film*

for lack of words to describe the new.

The Locomotive Act of 1865, also known as the Red Flag Act, due to its stipulation that any self-propelled road vehicle had to be preceded by a person walking at least 60 yards ahead, carrying a red flag, brought into force the world's first road speed limit: 4-mph in the country, 2-mph in towns, and a £10 fine for "speeding."[fig6-1] It was repealed four years later, on 14 November 1896, when the flag was scrapped and the speed limit was raised to 14-mph. Surely we can learn from such examples.

What we need in the future is to create new AI traffic rules which match with "wetware intelligence." The project that I worked on with Mr. Eno was called The Ship, in reference to the Titanic, the classic symbol of social and technological hubris. The "unsinkable" Titanic sank in 1912 and was followed by the sinking of Europe into WWI. The Ship project started in 2016, the year of Brexit, and President Trump's inauguration. It certainly pained many of us at that time, that the Internet, which so many of us had expected to make the world a more open and understanding place, was so easily weaponized to exacerbate our divisions.

We created a website using an AI image recognition model to search historical photo archives seeking references to news photos on real-time SNS.[fig6-2] The search results were displayed on a screen via excruciatingly slow transitions, a dream state of history repeating, a "nightmare we are trying to awaken from." The AI had not been trained for history or morality, or any particular point of view. It simply sought superficial similarities. Sometimes the juxtapositions were provocative. I remember photographs of prisoners of war on all fours matched with park benches. Partly because the work was produced in the midst of the Donald Trump vs. Hillary Clinton US presidential election, images of political rallies were prevalent, both Adolf Hitler and Rev. Martin Luther King before enthusiastic crowds. Our aim was to create an experience of uncanny bewilderment, incomprehension, and helplessness, witness to the non-sense of history presented sans narrative structure, or sense of history. Eno said he was interested in Artificial Stupidity: "I am, in fact, interested in taking advantage of the Artificial Stupidity inherent in computers. Computers often make weird and provocative mistakes that I would never have thought of. The character of every era is captured in the shortcomings of its technologies." I think we achieved it.

The phrase "artificial stupidity" disparages mal-appropriate AI, but I prefer to see all AI mistakes as interesting because they inform our preconceptions and shared bias. At the risk of overstating, my belief is that if traditional methodologies are the right answer, then innovative expressions and ideas start with "mistakes." Each evolution in creativity, from Picasso to DJs scratching vinyl has arguably begun as "mistakes." AI "mistakes" are neither "good" nor "bad" until they encounter our sense of utility. Algorithms are hypotheses. It is our responsibility to update them to better target "appropriate search space" and "evaluation function."

For me, the ideal heuristic for establishing a relationship with AI is found in the metaphor of surfing. The mystery of surfing is in how it can only function at the cusp of active and passive participation. Obviously, it is an activity predicated on ocean waves. But as a surfer, you are constantly in both a passive state of being at the mercy of the tides and an active mode of selecting which surge to ride. In order to identify a ride-appropriate wave you need experience, timing and effort to paddle out to the point where the wave breaks. The larger the break, the harder it is to paddle to. Knowing where to wait, and which wave to select, all have to be part of your recognition flow. In some ways, you've acceded control, in others you momentarily reclaim it. The unique experience of co-existing with the waves' own initiative is fundamental to the joy of surfing.

The phrase "surfing with AI" is meant to function as a metaphor for how AI similarly requires you to discover an active/passive mindset, a recognition of vast quantities of data, and which anomalies, or patterns to use in pursuit of provocative unexpectedness. After each such "surfing" session, it's important to dis-board, stand on one's own two feet on solid land, and update one's evaluation criteria. I assume that this attitude applies to areas other than "creation" and "expression." I assume that there may be similar experiences to be found in other sports, such as martial arts, or dance.

A society's wealth and culture are the results of choices its members make regarding when to seize and relinquish control, and how they strategically employ AI. For someone like me who is not good at driving, the steering wheel of a car is a control I want to accede immediately. The world is a safer place with AI instead of me at the wheel. But I would never allow AI to control my informational diet. I want to navigate those waves, and not be subsumed by them. Leaving everything to AI is not a path to happiness. Rather, it is our individual differences which give richness to AI, and to our lives.

Endnotes

1. Cyril Diagne, Nicolas Barradeau, Simon Doury, *t-SNE Map*, Experiments with Google (2018) https://experiments.withgoogle.com/t-sne-map
2. In the process of a CNN learning photo data, background and foreground context is often used. In Janel Shane's book *You Look Like a Thing and I Love You: How Artificial Intelligence Works and Why It's Making the World a Weirder Place* (Little, Brown and Company, 2019) a CNN is mentioned which had correctly recognized a picture with sheep grazing in the grassland, but which then mistook the sheep for giraffe or birds after the picture had been edited to place the sheep in a tree.
3. Other dimensionality reduction algorithms include well-known PCA (Principal Component Analysis) and UMAP (Uniform Manifold Approximation and Projection).
4. *Graphic design co-created with AI*, Tokyo Midtown Design Hub
https://designhub.jp/exhibitions/4564/
5. Mario Klingemann, Simon Doury, *X Degrees of Separation,* Experiments with Google (2018)
https://experiments.withgoogle.com/x-degrees-of-separation
6. Aya Saito, *Why Humans Draw Pictures-Invitation to Art and Cognitive Science* (Iwanami Shoten, 2014)
7. *The AI DJ Project — A dialogue between AI and a human,*
https://www.qosmo.jp/en/art/ai-dj-human-dj-b2b is a collaboration with Mr. Shoya Dozono, who kindly provided the wonderful graphics on the cover of this book.
8. A project for the event 2045, which began as a collaboration with Daito Manabe, of Rhizomatiks.
9. Via (Torema, 2007), a DVD featuring Japanese techno DJ pioneer Fumiya Tanaka wearing a headset and verbalizing his thought process while DJing.
10. The latest version has been modified to include a Variational Auto-encoder for more consistent music distribution.
11. This mechanism is based on the following paper: Len Vande Veire, Tijl De Bie, *From raw audio to a seamless mix: creating an automated DJ system for Drum and Bass*, EURASIP Journal on Audio, Speech, and Music Processing (2018)
12. This technology smoothes the connection between songs by matching the tempo and rhythm between songs in transitions. DJs working with vinyl record or CD sound sources needs to manually adjust such parameters with a pitch controller while listening to both.
13. After that, AI played the techno song I played during the rehearsal, so I tried to steal my AI's idea. I intended to play the jazz song it chose, but I mistakenly played the flip side of the record, a completely different song which provided more cold sweat than goosebumps.
14. Jordan Ferguson, *The Beat Revolution of J. Dila and Donuts* (DUBOOKS, 2018)
15. Davide Sciortino, *Why Would You Quantize All of This - J Dilla: The Perception of Groove and the Re-Definition of Hip Hop and Electronic Beat*, The Institute of Contemporary Music Performance (University of East London, 04.2014)
16. *5 Things We Learned From ?uestlove at RBMA* (2017)
https://www.redbull.com/us-en/5-things-we-learned-from-questlove
17. *M4L.RhythmVAE: VAE Rhythm Generator for Ableton Live*, Computational Creativity Lab (Keio University SFC)
https://cclab.sfc.keio.ac.jp/projects/m4l-rhythmvae/
18. *Ilsrael Galvan + YCAM, Israel & イスラエル*, Yamaguchi Center for Arts and Media (2019)
https://www.ycam.jp/events/2019/israel-and-israel/
19. Like the *M4L.RhythmVAE*, this plug-in uses an architecture called a Variational Auto-encoder (VAE).

20. Kevin Kelly, *The Myth of a Superhuman AI* (WIRED, 04.2017)
    https://www.wired.com/2017/04/the-myth-of-a-superhuman-ai/
    Kelly's argument is more about the value of heterogeneity. My take is that it is a form of "Alien Intelligence."
21. Most of the AI-based works covered in this book fall into the category of art based on generative and unpredictable behavior, by systems that operate according to algorithms and rules. In a more narrow sense, it may also refer to visual work that uses programming.
    Jason Bailey *Why Love Generative Art?* (Artnome, 08.2018)
    https://www.artnome.com/news/2018/8/8/why-love-generative-art
22. *Dribnet* https://drib.net
23. Another aspect to the (legendary formulator of the Japanese tea ceremony as we know it today, advisor to successive Daimyo, and priest) Sen no Rikyu is that he was the owner of a fish wholesaling enterprise in Sakai city. The reason why he used the fish basket in a tea ceremony example is presumed to be for its vernacular associations.
    Genpei Akasegawa, *Senrikyu-Silent Avant-garde* (Iwanami Shoten, 1990)
24. Aya Saito, *Why Humans Draw Pictures-Invitation to Art and Cognitive Science* (Iwanami Shoten, 2014)
25. Shinseungback Kimyonghun, *Nonfacial Portrait* (2018)
    http://ssbkyh.com/works/nonfacial_portrait/
26. Google AI Blog, *Inceptionism: Going Deeper into Neural Networks* (06.2015)
    https://blog.research.google/2015/06/inceptionism-going-deeper-into-neural.html
27. Ian J. Goodfellow, Jonathon Shlens, Christian Szegedy, *Explaining and Harnessing Adversarial Examples* / arXiv: 1412.6572v3 [stat.ML] (03.2015)
28. Shin Amano, Eiko Hirata, Ryosuke Nakajima, Yuka Sai, Naoki Tanaka, Risako Kawashima, and Nao Tokui, *UNLABELED – Camouflage against the machines* (2019)
    A research project created in collaboration with Dentsu Lab Tokyo.
    https://cclab.sfc.keio.ac.jp/projects/unlabeled/
29. A play on clothing brands being called labels.
30. For the comparison between architects and gardeners, refer to the following article.
    Brian Eno, *Composers as Gardeners* (Edge.Org, 2011)
    https://www.edge.org/conversation/brian_eno-composers-as-gardeners
31. "I can't even feel it, I'm going to call it the outside, the other side I don't know. Creation is about accepting what comes from the outside."
    Yukio Gunji Pegio, *Natural Intelligence* (Kodansha, 2019)

Afterword

I'm done. At last! Thank you for joining me on this adventure.

I started writing this to summarize what I've learned about AI and creativity. Richard Feynman said If you can't explain an idea to an 8-year-old, you don't understand it. I tried to explain AI, not to 8 year-olds, but at least to non-specialists. But the process was really useful to me, for articulating a lot of ideas from throughout my career.

I have one of those jobs that nobody has a clear picture of, myself included. I work in music. I work in media art. I worked as a university researcher, and now I lecture as part of a university faculty. I also run a company. For me, it all begins from an interest in "processes": how ideas mutate and metamorphose, and how to identify moments when different means of output arise, in different forms, for different mediums. There's the problem again. Strange phrases, like the one I just made, have always been clear to me, within this "occupation," this strange complex of things that I do. But did that make sense to you, dear reader?

I used to say I did Meta-art, in a nod to Harold Cohen. I sometimes call myself an artist, embracing Marshall McLuhan's "Art is anything you can get away with." But does the artistic community at large embrace me as one of their own? Am I just making excuses? That's not my intention. My point is that many of us today are working in fast-evolving new creative fields which are still really poorly defined. That's the nature of rapid change, which AI will continue to accelerate. 20 years into my career of these "process-oriented" things, I found myself completely ill-equipped to explain to or share how my thinking and activities represent my occupation.

Then, in 2018, I was invited to do a lecture series at Ikegami Laboratory, an Artificial Life research facility at the University of Tokyo. I prepared what became the basis for this book *An Introduction to Computational Creativity*. A tweet of my outline caught the eye of editor and subcultural maven Gabin Ito, who introduced it to the editorial department at BNN, publishers of the Japanese edition. By the end of the lecture series, the book had already been commissioned. Around that same time, I was asked to join the faculty at Keio University SFC, and the learning curve to become a University professor took all of my energy. Even collecting the material to get started took a year.

Now as a non-tenured associate professor, I need more than ever to create a book, so that my students can understand what I can offer. In March 2020, as the extent of the threat posed by COVID-19 came into view, I shifted to remote work, both at my company and my university, which gave me more discretion about how I might spend my time. Whatever the reason, my writing engine kicked in. Since starting my company more than a decade ago, my focus had been on how to best work in a team. Suddenly working alone gave me the opportunity to shift gears, and focus on myself.

I often encourage students who seem unsure of their direction by saying, "Try getting swept away in your own ideas." I often get strange looks when I say this. Hopefully now they'll know what I mean.

The list of thanks is long, and I apologize in advance to anyone I may have omitted. I owe so much to so many. But I will start the list with Gabin Ito, who expressed interest in what I was doing long before there was a reasonable basis for it. Next I would like to express my sincerest gratitude to Sayaka Ishii of the BNN editorial department, Kazushi Kono, the assistant editor, and Junichi Murata, the editor-in-chief, for patiently dealing with an author who was inexperienced, and slow to deliver. Yurie Hata, who was in charge of the design of this book including binding, and Shoya Dozono, who was a collaborator in the AI DJ project and produced and provided the graphics for the cover and chapter doors. Any book is the product of a team, its merits should be shared by all, any faults belong solely to me.

I'd also like to thank my colleagues at Qosmo for redistributing our work load when I announced that I would begin teaching at university, and then again in writing this book. Also my friends at Dentsu Craft Tokyo, my students at my Computational Creativity Lab at Keio University SFC. The core of this book has been bettered by various projects and discussions that we have shared.

I would like to express my sincere gratitude to everyone at YCAM (Yamaguchi Center for Arts and Media) who worked with me on the AI DJ and collaboration project with Israel Galván. I stayed in Yamaguchi for a total of four months in 2018 and 2019, but thanks to everyone's hospitality and experimental spirit (not to forget hot springs, delicious sake and fish "gyoroque"), both were fun and fulfilling projects.

In this book, or rather, in my creative life, Brian Eno, Kevin Kelly, and Richard Dawkins have always had major impacts on my intellectual development. In particular, Brian Eno has inspired me not only by his view of music and art, but also by his outlook on life. His *Music for Airports* and *Reflection* continue to be my defaults for concentration. I cannot thank Kaoru Sugano of Dentsu enough for creating the opportunity to work with him.

XD program faculty members working on unknown designs at SFC, especially Shinya Fujii and Patrick Savage at the X-Music Lab, my colleagues in music research and production. I would also like to thank Kazuhiro Shiro, Dominick Chen, Kenichi Uryu, and Taro Yabuki for their comments on the manuscript at the galley stage. Mr. Yabuki, a laboratory alumnus, gave particularly detailed feedback. Discussions with each have added depth to the book. I would like to say in advance that I have referred to their knowledge and ideas, but repeat that any inadequacies in this book are solely the result of my own shortcomings.

The people who got me out of the house during the corona lockdown were neighborhood surfing companions Yohei Nakamichi, Masatomo Kobayashi, Naoki Tanaka, and Akihiro Otsuka, and without that time sharing the waves, this book would never have been completed.

Finally, I would like to express my sincere gratitude to my parents and family. My interest in natural science and technology was nurtured by my father, a junior high school science teacher, and I credit my joy of writing to my mother, whose specialty is elementary writing education.

Japanese society has long been said to lack individual creativity. As the COVID-19 pandemic inadvertently revealed, sometimes individual common sense is not the same as community sensibility. As AI permeates society, with whatever "disruptions" it may bring, I hope more people gain the consciousness to hang loose and ride the waves of the times together, along with AI, so that heterogeneous intelligence can increase.

Nao Tokui
November 2020,
Chigasaki, Japan.

Image Credits

Chapter 1

[fig1-1] Author (Illustration: Yurie Hata)
[fig1-2] Author (Illustration: Yurie Hata)
[fig1-3] Author
[fig1-4] Public Domain
[fig1-5] Public Domain
[fig1-6] Public Domain / WikiArt
[fig1-7] Above: Public Domain Below: Quoted from Goodfellow, Ian, Jean Pouget-Abadie, Mehdi Mirza, Bing Xu, David Warde-Farley, Sherjil Ozair, Aaron Courville, and Yoshua Bengio. 2020. "Generative Adversarial Networks." Communications of the ACM 63 (11): 139–44.
[fig1-8] Public Domain
[fig1-9] Public Domain
[fig1-10] Courtesy of Google
[fig1-11] Flintmi, Grand Wizzard Theodore, CC BY-SA 3.0 / Wikimedia Commons https://commons.wikimedia.org/wiki/File:Grand_wizzard_theodore.JPG

Chapter 2

[fig2-1] Left: Fair use / Wikipedia https://en.wikipedia.org/wiki/File:The_library_of_babel_-_bookcover.jpg Right: Erik Desmazières, Library of Congress
[fig2-2] Brandon Daniel, CC BY-SA 2.0 / Wikimedia Commons https://commons.wikimedia.org/wiki/File:Roland_TR-808(large).jpg
[fig2-3] Author (Illustration: Yurie Hata)
[fig2-4] Author (Illustration: Yurie Hata)
[fig2-5] Author (Illustration: Yurie Hata)
[fig2-7] Author (Illustration: Yurie Hata)
[fig2-8] Public Domain
[fig2-9] Fair use / Wikipedia
[fig2-10] Author (Illustration: Yurie Hata)
[fig2-11] Courtesy of Janelle Shane
[fig2-12] Public Domain
[fig2-13] Author (Illustration: Yurie Hata)
[fig2-14] Author. Based on a diagram in Oore, Sageev, Ian Simon, Sander Dieleman, Douglas Eck, and Karen Simonyan. 2020. "This Time with Feeling: Learning Expressive Musical Performance." Neural Computing & Applications 32 (4): 955–67.
[fig2-15] Author
[fig2-16] Author (Illustration: Yurie Hata)
[fig2-17] Public Domain
[fig2-18] Science Museum London, Babbage's Analytical Engine, CC BY-SA 2.0 https://commons.wikimedia.org/wiki/File:Babbages_Analytical_Engine,_1834-1871._(9660574685).jpg
[fig2-19] Public Domain
[fig2-20] Public Domain
[fig2-21] Public Domain
[fig2-22] Public Domain
[fig2-23] Takashi Otaka, Courtesy of NTT Intercommunication Center [ICC]
[fig2-24] Courtesy of NTT Intercommunication Center [ICC]
[fig2-25] Courtesy of Karl Sims
[fig2-26] Karl Sims, Evolving Virtual Creatures / SIGGRAPH '94: Proceedings of the 21st annual conference on Computer graphics and interactive techniques (07.1994)
[fig2-27] Author, Screenshots of https://gatc.ca/projects/biomorphevolve/
[fig2-28] Author
[fig2-29] Author (Illustration: Yurie Hata). Based on Ahmed Elgammal, Bingchen Liu, Mohamed Elhoseiny, Marian Mazzone, CAN: Creative Adversarial Networks, Generating "Art" by Learning About Styles and Deviating from Style Norms / arXiv:1706.07068v1 [cs.AI] (2017)
[fig2-30] Quoted from Elgammal et al.

Chapter 3

[fig3-1] Frank S Macomber, The Sound of Fame: Syracuse University's Audio Archive and Edison Re-Recording Laboratory
[fig3-2] Public Domain
[fig3-3] Public Domain
[fig3-4] ZERO–G
[fig3-5] CC BY-SA 1.0 / Wikimedia Commons https://commons.wikimedia.org/wiki/File:Roland_TB-303_Panel.jpg
[fig3-6] Public Domain
[fig3-7] Public Domain
[fig3-8] Public Domain
[fig3-9] Public Domain
[fig3-10] Public Domain
[fig3-11] Public Domain
[fig3-12] Public Domain
[fig3-13] Public Domain
[fig3-14] Public Domain
[fig3-15] Above: Man Ray, Fair Use/WikiArt https://www.wikiart.org/en/manray/dora-marr Left: Pablo Picasso, Fair Use/WikiArt https://www.wikiart.org/en/pablo-picasso/portrait-of-doramaar-1937-1 Right: Courtesy of Michael McNaughtonn
[fig3-16] Rights Managed, Robotic artist producing a painting, SCIENCEphotoLIBRARY
[fig3-17] Above: Harold Cohen, V&A Collections http://collections.vam.ac.uk/item/O499574/amsterdam-suite-f-printcohen-harold/ Below (from left to right): Georg Nees, V&A collections http://collections.vam.ac.uk/item/O221321/schotter-print-nees-georg/ | Frieder Nake, V&A collections http://collections.vam.ac.uk/item/O211685/hommage-a-paul-klee-13965-print-nake-frieder/ | Manfred Mohr, V&A collections http://collections.vam.ac.uk/item/O154610/p-197-print-mohrmanfred/

[fig3-18] Harold Cohen, V&A Collections
http://collections.vam.ac.uk/item/O499587/drawing-cohen-harold/

Chapter 4

[fig4-1] AP Photo - Steven Senne, Matt O'Brien, Face recognition researcher fights Amazon over biased AI, Associated Press News
https://apnews.com/article/24fd8e9bc6bf485c8aff1e46ebde9ec1
[fig4-2] @Chicken3gg(Twitter)
[fig4-3] Author (Illustration: Yurie Hata)
[fig4-4] Courtesy of Peter Chilvers
[fig4-5] CC By 2.0/flickr
https://www.flickr.com/photos/blakespot/48315444592/in/photostream/
[fig4-6] Author (Illustration: Yurie Hata)
[fig4-7] Author (Illustration: Yurie Hata)

Chapter 5

[fig5-1] Cyril Diagne, Nicolas Barradeau, Simon Doury
[fig5-2] Image used in the figure: Chris Olah, Alexander Mordvintsev, and Ludwig Schubert, Feature Visualization, CC BY-4.0
https://distill.pub/2017/featurevisualization/
[fig5-3] t-SNE Map
https://artsexperiments.withgoogle.com/tsnemap/#3497.78,214.07,4499.54,3425.43,0.00,4642.30
[fig5-4] t-SNE Map,
https://artsexperiments.withgoogle.com/tsnemap/#1803.70,174.96,4970.90,2065.24,0.00,5201.92
[fig5-5] JAGDA Internet Committee, Qosmo
[fig5-6] Mario Klingemann, Simon Doury
[fig5-7] Rakutaro Ogiwara
[fig5-8] Author (Illustration: Yurie Hata)
[fig5-9] Author
[fig5-10] Author
[fig5-11] Author (Illustration: Yurie Hata)
[fig5-12] Google
[fig5-13] Yasuhiro Tani, Courtesy of Yamaguchi Center for Arts and Media [YCAM]
[fig5-14] Public Domain
[fig5-15] Author
[fig5-16] Tomoki Moriya, Courtesy of Yamaguchi Center for Arts and Media [YCAM]
[fig5-17] CC BY 2.0, Abalg, Israel Galván, Wikimedia Commons
https://commons.wikimedia.org/wiki/File:Israel_Galván.jpg
[fig5-18] Author. I am obliged to Mitsuto Ando for his many contributions to the production of the boots and the computer-controlled turntable for AI DJ.
[fig5-19] Tomoki Moriya, Courtesy of Yamaguchi Center for Arts and Media [YCAM]
[fig5-20] Author
[fig5-21] Courtesy of Tom White
[fig5-22] Public Domain
[fig5-23] Courtesy of Shinseungback Kimyonghun
[fig5-24] Public Domain
[fig5-25] Author
[fig5-26] Quoted from Ian J. Goodfellow, Jonathon Shlens, Christian Szegedy, Explaining and Harnessing Adversarial Examples / arXiv: 1412.6572v3 [stat.ML] (03.2015)
[fig5-27] Ryo Hanamoto

Chapter 6

[fig6-1] Public Domain
[fig6-2] Dentsu Lab Tokyo

Profile

Nao Tokui
Artist / Researcher, Ph.D. (Engineering)

Nao Tokui is an artist, DJ, AI technology researcher, and visiting associate professor at Keio University, Tokyo. After completing his Ph.D., in 2009, he founded the AI Creativity and Music Lab Qosmo, Inc. Their works have been exhibited at venues including The Museum of Modern Art (MoMA), New York, and the Barbican Centre, London. Their performances employing AI have been showcased at music festivals including MUTEK and Sónar. He is currently leading development of AI technologies for audio creators at his new firm Neutone Inc.

Surfing human creativity with AI — A user's guide

Translation: David d'Heilly
Proofreading: 湯浅し津 Shizu Yuasa, Jeff Kim, Marcos Alonso
Book design: 畑ユリエ Yurie Hata
Cover Illustration: 堂園翔矢 Shoya Dozono
Management: 安江沙希子 Sakiko Yasue

Title: 創るためのAI — 機械と創造性のはてしない物語
Tsukuru tameno AI — Kikai to Souzousei no Hateshinai Monogatari

Author: 徳井直生 Nao Tokui
Publisher of Japanese edition: BNN
Japanese Edition Publication Date: January 20, 2021
ISBN: 978-4-8025-1200-8

www.ingramcontent.com/pod-product-compliance
Lightning Source LLC
Chambersburg PA
CBHW072138170526
45158CB00004BA/1417